CU00926381

THE CHRONICLES OF

CONAN®

VOLUME 10

WHEN GIANTS WALK THE EARTH
AND OTHER STORIES

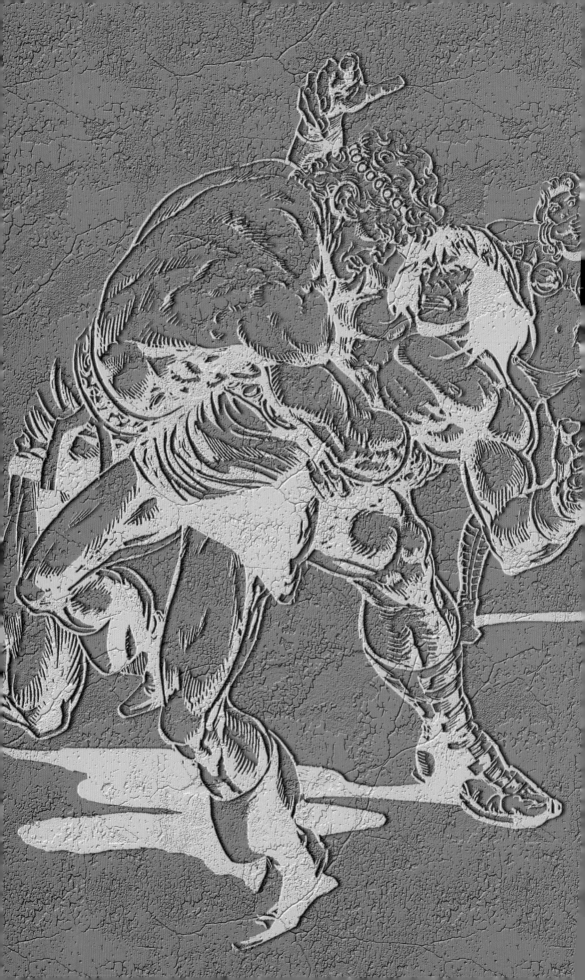

THE CHRONICLES OF
CONAN
VOLUME 10

WHEN GIANTS WALK THE EARTH
AND OTHER STORIES

based on the classic pulp
character Conan the Barbarian,
created by

ROBERT E. HOWARD

written by

ROY THOMAS

illustrated by

JOHN BUSCEMA,
HOWARD CHAYKIN,
and others

coloring by

**PETER DAWES, IAN SOKOLIWSKI,
DENNIS KASHTON,** and **WIL GLASS** with
ALL THUMBS CREATIVE

DARK HORSE BOOKS™

publisher
MIKE RICHARDSON

collection designer
M. JOSHUA ELLIOTT

art director
LIA RIBACCHI

collection editor
JEREMY BARLOW

Special thanks to Fredrik Malmberg and Thommy Wojciechowski at
Conan Properties; Arthur Lieberman at Lieberman & Norwalk,LLP;
Marco Lupoi at Panini; Scott Allie, Kurt Busiek, Lance Kreiter,
and Roy Thomas.

This volume collects issues seventy-two through seventy-seven, and seventy-nine through
eighty-two of the Marvel comic-book series **Conan the Barbarian**.

THE CHRONICLES OF CONAN®: WHEN GIANTS WALK THE EARTH AND OTHER STORIES
The Chronicles of Conan®: When Giants Walk the Earth and other stories. ©1975, 2006 Conan Properties
International, LLC. Conan® and Conan the Barbarian® (including all prominent characters featured in this
issue) and the distinctive likenesses thereof are trademarks of Conan Properties International, LLC unless
otherwise noted. Text and illustration © Conan Properties International, LLC, all other material ©Dark
Horse Comics. Dark Horse Books™ is a trademark of Dark Horse Comics, Inc. Dark Horse Comics® is a
trademark of Dark Horse Comics, Inc., registered in various categories and countries. All rights reserved.
No portion of this publication may be reproduced or transmitted, in any form or by any means, without the
express written permission of Dark Horse Comics, Inc. Names, characters, places, and incidents featured in
this publication either are the product of the author's imagination or are used fictitiously. Any resemblance
to actual persons (living or dead), events, institutions, or locales, without satiric intent, is coincidental.

Published by Dark Horse Books
A division of Dark Horse Comics, Inc.
10956 SE Main Street
Milwaukie, OR 97222

www.darkhorse.com
www.conan.com

To find a comics shop in your area, call the Comic Shop Locator Service
toll-free at 1-888-266-4226

First edition March 2006
ISBN: 1-59307-490-5

1 3 5 7 9 10 8 6 4 2

Printed in China

TABLE OF CONTENTS

ALL STORIES WRITTEN BY ROY THOMAS

"Know, O prince, that between the years when the oceans drank Atlantis and the gleaming cities, and the rise of the sons of Aryas, there was an Age undreamed of, when shining kingdoms lay spread across the world like blue mantles beneath the stars.

"Hither came Conan, the Cimmerian, black-haired, sullen-eyed, sword in hand, a thief, a reaver, a slayer, with gigantic melancholies and gigantic mirth, to tread the jeweled thrones of the Earth under his sandaled feet."

—The Nemedian Chronicles.

STAN LEE PRESENTS: CONAN THE BARBARIAN ™

VENGEANCE IN ASGALUN

"THERE IS SCANT PROFIT IN TRADE WITH THE FIERCE AND WARY SONS OF SHEM!" SO RUNS AN OLD HYBORIAN PROVERB.

"IN AND AT THEM, BROTHERS!"

THROW DOWN YOUR SWORDS, DOGS--OR DIE!!

THERE IS EVEN LESS TO SHOW FOR IT WHEN A SHEMITE MERCHANT VESSEL IS BOARDED BY THE FIERCE BLACK CORSAIRS, UNDER THE LEADERSHIP OF THE SHE-PIRATE BÊLIT AND HER WILD-EYED LOVER, CONAN THE CIMMERIAN--!

ROY THOMAS & JOHN BUSCEMA
AUTHOR/EDITOR   ILLUSTRATOR

ERNIE CHAN, EMBELLISHER

J. COSTANZA LETTERER

FEATURING THE CREATIONS OF ROBERT E. HOWARD

7

THE BELEAGUERED *SHEMITES* SPURRED ON BY THEIR DUTY-CONSCIOUS *CAPTAIN,* DO *NOT* TOSS DOWN THEIR SWORDS, AS THEY HAVE BEEN BADE...

AND, A MOMENT LATER, AS MORE THAN 200 POUNDS OF *HURTLING BARBARIAN* STRIKES THEM-- THEY HAVE AMPLE REASON TO *REGRET* THAT INACTION!

THE *CAPTAIN,* HOWEVER, HAS NO TIME TO *RECONSIDER* HIS DECISION--

FOR, HE IS THE *NEXT* TO FALL BEFORE CONAN'S FLASHING SWORD!

GAARRRH

NOR IS *BÊLIT* SLOW TO *NOTE* THE FACT:

ALL RIGHT, MY CORSAIRS-- THEIR CAPTAIN'S *DEAD,* AND ALL HOPE *LOST!*

THE FIGHT WILL GO *OUT* OF THEM NOW, AND *SWIFTLY.*

LET ANY WHO WILL, *SURRENDER--* AND DON'T *SLAY* ANY MAN WHO CHOOSES TO HURL DOWN HIS *SWORD!*

AYE, GODDESS! WE HEAR AND *OBEY.*

ONE EBON-SKINNED BOARDER, HOWEVER, CHOOSES NEITHER TO HEAR *NOR* TO OBEY...

YOU PALE *JACKAL--!*

NO--DON'T! I-I SURRENDER--!

TELL THAT TO *DAGON* AND *DERKETA*, WHEN YOU CRAWL INTO THEIR PRESENCE IN *HELL!*

NO--NO--!!

KAWAKU!

IS SOMETHING *WRONG*, GODDESS?

YOU KNOW DAMNED *WELL* SOMETHING IS WRONG, YOU ARROGANT DEVIL!

DIDN'T YOU HEAR ME YELL TO *SPARE* ANY WHO CHOSE TO *YIELD?*

NO, GODDESS. THEY ARE ALL ENEMIES-- *SHEMITES*--!

I AM A SHEMITE, *TOO* -- OR HAVE YOU *FORGOTTEN?*

DO YOU LUST PERHAPS TO SPILL *MY* BLOOD AS FREELY AS YOU DID MY *COUNTRYMAN'S?*

N-NO, GODDESS! I *SWEAR* I--

LYING PIG!

I *LET* YOU CORSAIRS VENT YOUR SPLEEN ON THOSE DEVIL-DOGS, THE *STYGIANS*-- AYE, AND EVEN ON SOME *HYBORIAN* SHIPS--

BUT, THE SHIPS OF *SHEM* ARE TO BE *LOOTED* ONLY, WITH A *MINIMUM* OF BLOODSHED.

YOU WILL *REMEMBER* THAT NEXT TIME, WON'T YOU, KAWAKU?

AYE, GODDESS-- I SHALL REMEMBER THAT.

THAT... AND MUCH MORE...!

THE FIGHT *ENDED* NOW, THE GOLDEN *GUTS* OF THE SHEMITE VESSEL ARE QUICKLY REMOVED, AND THE CRAFT SENT LIMPING *NORTHWARD.*

SO, WOMAN-- MORE *SHEMITE COINS*, WHICH WILL IN TIME PAY FOR *MERCENARY TROOPS* TO RECONQUER YOUR THRONE IN *ASGALUN*, EH?

AYE! WHILE THAT TRAITOR *NIM-KARRAK* WEARS THE CROWN OF MY HOME CITY-- MY *UNCLE*, THE MURDERER OF MY *FATHER* WHEN I WAS BUT A *CHILD*--

--THERE IS *NO HOME* FOR BÊLIT, NOT EVEN THE ROLLING *SEA.*

THERE NEVER *HAS* BEEN.

GODDESS! WHAT'S *WRONG,* YASUNGA? YOU WERE TO TEND TO *N'YAGA* DURING THE FRAY.

OUT OF MY *WAY!*

I *DID,* GODDESS! BUT-- HE IS *MORE SICK* THAN BEFORE. HE--

I MUST *GO* TO HIM!

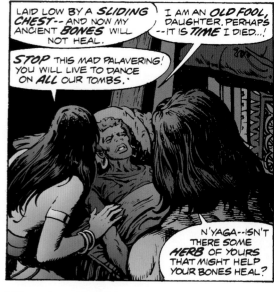

LAID LOW BY A *SLIDING CHEST*-- AND NOW MY ANCIENT *BONES* WILL NOT HEAL.

I AM AN *OLD FOOL,* DAUGHTER. PERHAPS --IT IS *TIME* I DIED...!

STOP THIS MAD PALAVERING! YOU WILL LIVE TO DANCE ON *ALL OUR* TOMBS.

N'YAGA--ISN'T THERE SOME *HERB* OF YOURS THAT MIGHT HELP YOUR BONES HEAL?

HERB? AYE--THERE *WAS* AN HERB-- I EXTRACTED A *POWDER* FROM IT THAT WOULD HELP--

BUT, THERE IS ONLY *ONE VIAL* OF IT LEFT NOW--

THEN I'LL *GET* IT FOR YOU! WHERE *IS* IT?

IN THE *ROYAL PALACE...* AT *ASGALUN.*

WHAT??

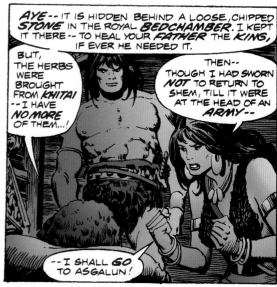

AYE-- IT IS HIDDEN BEHIND A LOOSE, CHIPPED *STONE* IN THE ROYAL *BEDCHAMBER.* I KEPT IT THERE -- TO HEAL YOUR *FATHER* THE *KING,* IF EVER HE NEEDED IT.

BUT, THE HERBS WERE BROUGHT FROM *KHITAI* -- I HAVE *NO MORE* OF THEM...!

THEN-- THOUGH I HAD SWORN *NOT* TO RETURN TO SHEM, TILL IT WERE AT THE HEAD OF AN *ARMY*--

--I SHALL *GO* TO ASGALUN!

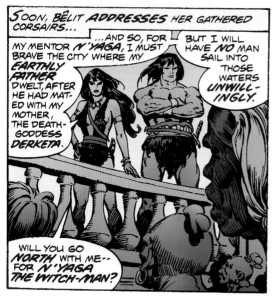

SOON, BÊLIT ADDRESSES HER GATHERED CORSAIRS...

...AND SO, FOR MY MENTOR *N'YAGA,* I MUST BRAVE THE CITY WHERE MY *EARTHLY FATHER* DWELT, AFTER HE HAD MATED WITH MY MOTHER, THE DEATH- GODDESS *DERKETA.*

BUT I WILL HAVE *NO MAN* SAIL INTO THOSE WATERS *UNWILLINGLY.*

WILL YOU GO *NORTH* WITH ME-- FOR *N'YAGA* THE *WITCH-MAN?*

ALMOST AS ONE MAN, THE EBONY WARRIORS RAISE THEIR VOICES IN A GREAT SHOUT...

AYE! AYE! FOR N'YAGA-- AND FOR BÊLIT!!

BUT ONE MAN IS SILENT: KAWAKU, WHOM MEN CALL THE CRAVEN ONE.

BÉLIT'S mind, however, is elsewhere...

AND YOU, MY BARBARIAN? I CANNOT ASK YOU TO RISK YOUR LIFE FOR AN OLD SHAMAN -- BUT ONLY YOU, OF ALL ABOARD, COULD ACCOMPANY ME ASHORE.

IF YOU HADN'T ASKED ME, WOMAN...

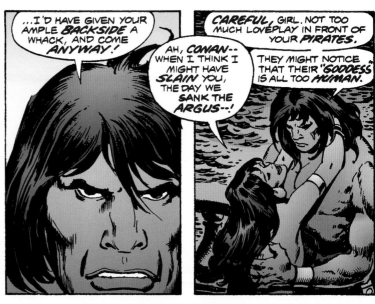

...I'D HAVE GIVEN YOUR AMPLE BACKSIDE A WHACK, AND COME ANYWAY!

AH, CONAN-- WHEN I THINK I MIGHT HAVE SLAIN YOU, THE DAY WE SANK THE ARGUS--!

CAREFUL, GIRL. NOT TOO MUCH LOVEPLAY IN FRONT OF YOUR PIRATES.

THEY MIGHT NOTICE THAT THEIR "GODDESS" IS ALL TOO HUMAN.

THUS, IN THE DAYS TO COME, THE SHIPPING LANES OFF THE BLACK COAST ARE SAFE FOR A TIME...

...AS THE TIGRESS HEADS NORTH.

SOON, THE JAGGED SHORELINE OF SHEM IS OFF THEIR STARBOARD PROW...

AND, ERE LONG, THEY PASS IN THE NIGHT BY THE WALLED CITY-STATE OF ASGALUN-- TOO DISDAINFUL OF SEA-TRADE TO HAVE SO MUCH AS A HARBOR.

JUST PAST DAWN, TWO STRIDENT FIGURES STALK GATEWARD, THEIR STEP BELYING THEIR MODEST APPAREL...

PLAGUE TAKE THESE SKIRTS!

I'VE NOT WORN SUCH A THING SINCE I WAS A CHILD.

YOU LOOK FINE.

PAH! THIS IS NOT THE WAY I INTENDED TO APPROACH THE GATES OF ASGALUN!

YOU KEEP SAYING.

WELL, WE'RE HERE-- SO REMEMBER, I'M A WEAPONS-MAKER, AND YOU'RE MY HUMBLE WIFE.

MITRA! HAVE THEY A DEAF GATEKEEPER?

I *HEAR* YOU, IN ISHTAR'S NAME! WHAT DO YE *WANT?*

ENTRANCE TO THE *CITY.*

WE'VE ALREADY *GOT* ALL THE PEOPLE WE *NEED.*

A CITY CAN *ALWAYS* USE ANOTHER GOOD *MAKER OF WEAPONS.*

WELLLL...AT LEAST YE'RE NOT *STYGIANS...*

WE'VE GOT FAR TOO MANY OF *THOSE* RIGHT NOW FOR *MY* LIKING.

MY *THANKS,* GATEKEEPER.

STYGIANS! AT THE VERY WORD, BÊLIT'S *SKIN* CRAWLS--

NOR DO THE SIGHTS SHE SOON SEES LESSEN HER HATRED...

THE *LOCALS* ARE GETTING FAR TOO *UPPITTY* FOR MY TASTES!

A NICK *KICK,* PTAMAN!

:OOOF--!:

SLINK BACK INTO YOUR *SHEMITE HOLES*--AND MAKE WAY FOR YOUR *STYGIAN BETTERS!*

STAND ASIDE, RABBLE!

CURSE THE DAY KING ATRAHASIS WAS SLAIN--

--AND *NIM-KARRAK* OPENED THE CITY TO *DEVILS FROM THE SOUTH!*

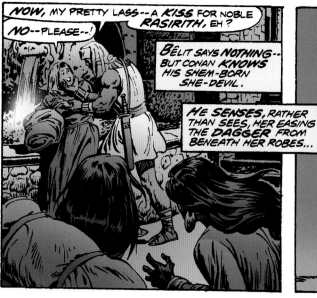

NOW, MY PRETTY LASS--A *KISS* FOR NOBLE *RASIRITH,* EH?

NO--PLEASE--!

BÊLIT SAYS NOTHING--BUT CONAN *KNOWS* HIS SHEM-BORN SHE-DEVIL.

HE SENSES, RATHER THAN SEES, HER EASING THE *DAGGER* FROM BENEATH HER ROBES...

AND HE ACTS AS NONCHALANTLY AS POSSIBLE, UNDER THE CIRCUMSTANCES.

OHH--!

AS BÊLIT HAS PREVIOUSLY *SAID*:

THIS IS *NOT* THE WAY SHE HAD *PLANNED* HER TRIUMPHAL RE-ENTRY INTO THE CITY OF HER ROYAL *BIRTH*.

YOU--YOU *TRIPPED* ME, YOU--!!

WHAT'S *THIS*? A PUBLIC *BRAWL*?

NO SUCH *THING*, MILORD.

MY GOOD *WIFE* AND I WERE MERELY *PRACTICING*, FOR YOUR *ENTERTAINMENT*.

YOU SEE, WE ARE...*ACROBATS*, AMONG OTHER THINGS...

...AND WE AIM TO *AMUSE*.

THEN YOU HAVE *FAILED* IN YOUR AIM: FOR I AM *NOT* AMUSED.

YES, MILORD.

TAKE YOUR *PEASANT* PAST-TIMES *ELSE-WHERE*, BEFORE I CART YOU OFF TO THE *DUNGEON*!

THANK YOU, MILORD.

...ANY MORE THAN THE *CIMMERIAN* SENSES THE MAKE-SHIFT *CLUB* DESCENDING ON HIS HARD *SKULL*...

UNNH--!

THE SCROWLING *STYGIAN* HARDLY *SUSPECTS* HOW CLOSE HE HAS COME TO *DEATH*...

...UNTIL *TOO LATE*!

THERE! SEND *ME* SPRAWLING IN THE MUD, WILL YOU, *HUSBAND*?

HAH! NOW *THAT'S* FUNNY!

I WAGER *PTOR-NUBIS* AND THE OTHER NOBLES AT THE *PALACE* WOULD LIKE IT, AS *WELL*!

PTOR-NUBIS? A *STYGIAN* NAME! I THOUGHT THIS WAS A *SHEMITE* CITY.

YOU'LL NOT THINK SO *LONG*, NOW THAT YOU'RE *HERE*.

YES, BY SET--I THINK I *WILL* TAKE YOU TO THE PALACE.

THIS IS *FAR* MORE AMUSING THAN THE *PUPPET SHOWS* THE LOCAL FOOLS PUT ON.

IT WAS *MEANT* TO BE...*MILORD*.

13

THUS, MOMENTS LATER, A *BARBARIAN* AND A *SHEMITE* RIDE IN UNACCUSTOMED *LUXURY* THRU THE STREETS OF ASGALUN--

--ASTRIDE A *CHARIOT* DRIVEN BY A *STYGIAN WARRIOR.*

AS THEY DO SO, *BÉLIT SEETHES* ALMOST VISIBLY; FOR, THESE ARE *HER* PEOPLE--OR *WOULD* HAVE BEEN, HAD HER *UNCLE* NOT SLAIN HER FATHER, WITH OLD *N'YAGA* CARRYING THE YOUNG PRINCESS TO *SAFETY.*

AS FOR *CONAN:* HE SEES NOW THAT THERE IS *MORE* THAN MERE DESIRE FOR *REVENGE* IN HIS MATE'S HEART.

THERE IS ALSO *PITY*--FOR A PEOPLE FALLING MORE AND MORE UNDER THE HARD *STYGIAN* YOKE.

SOON, AT THE MONOLITHIC *PALACE...*

CROM! THEY GROW STONE LIONS *BIG* HERE IN ASGALUN!

SILENCE, OUTLANDER! YOU WILL SPEAK ONLY WHEN *SPOKEN* TO--

--WHICH, IN THE *ROYAL COURT,* WILL BE *SELDOM.*

SO *THIS* IS WHERE YOU *GREW* UP.

AND WHERE MY *FATHER* WAS *SLAIN!*

O NIM-KARRAK, SOVEREIGN OF *ASGALUN--*

--AND *PTOR-NUBIS,* EMISSARY OF *CTESPHON II,* KING OF ALL *STYGIA,* MASTER OF THE *SUN-BOAT,* RIDER OF THE MOON-STEED--CONQUEROR OF ALL HE *BEHOLDS*--

BEHOLD THESE TWO *ACROBATS,* WHOM I HAVE SOUGHT OUT FOR THE *AMUSEMENT* OF YOUR COURT.

WELL DONE, RASIRITH. BUT, *NEXT* TIME, PLEASE REMEMBER THAT *I,* NOT DISTANT *CTESPHON,* AM KING HERE.

HE IS *AWARE* OF THAT, SIRE.

WELL--HE RECITES *YOUR* KING'S FULL REGALIA, AND PRECIOUS LITTLE OF *MINE!*

14

NO NEED FOR *BITTERNESS*, NIM-KARRAK.

YOU STILL HAVE THE *THRONE* YOU ALWAYS COVETED.

AYE--AND THE *MEREST SHADOW* OF REAL *POWER!*

I LIVE, I SLEEP, I *BREATHE* SURROUNDED BY *STYGIANS!* I--

SUDDENLY, THE KING *HALTS* HIS *TOO-FAMILIAR* TIRADE...

...UPON BEHOLDING THE *LOOK OF HATRED*, UNSUCCESSFULLY MASKED, UPON THE FACE OF THE *WOMAN* BEFORE HIM!

BÊLIT, HOWEVER, IS *NEW* TO THE WAYS OF *SOME* MEN.

SHE CANNOT KNOW THAT SUCH HATRED MERELY STIRS KIM-KARRAK'S *PASSIONS*.

IT IS *PTOR-NUBIS* WHO INTERRUPTS THE AWKWARD SILENCE...

WE COULD PERHAPS USE *BOTH* A BIT OF *DIVERSION,* IN OUR VARIOUS WAYS, O KING.

YOU *OUTLANDERS* --WHAT DO YOU *DO?*

DO, MILORD?

WHY ANYTHING WE *CAN*--

--AND RATHER *MORE* THAN WE *WANT* TO--

WH--?

--BUT *MOSTLY,* TRICKS LIKE *THIS!*

HOW *PHYSICAL.*

CONAN HAS LEARNED SOMETHING FROM HIS YOUNG FRIEND *TARA,* TILL RECENTLY AN *ACROBAT...*

BUT, HE HAS CHOSEN HIS *TIMING* BADLY-- FOR, FILLED WITH *HATRED* OF NIM-KARRAK, BÊLIT IS NO LONGER IN THE *MOOD* TO GO ALONG WITH THE *GAME...*

PUT ME *DOWN,* YOU *OAF!*

AS YOU *WISH,* MY DEAR.

UNABLE TO ALLAY THE *TENSION* RUNNING THRU THE *SHE-PIRATE...*

AND, WHEN HE ATTEMPTS TO *IGNORE* IT, BY BOWING IN HIS LEAST SERVILE MANNER BEFORE THE *USURPERS*...

SERPENTS OF SET!

...SHE GRABS A HANDY *SWORD*...

AND ONLY *CONAN* IS CERTAIN, IN THAT MOMENT, THAT IT IS *NOT* MEANT FOR *HIM*.

THEN, AS BÊLIT STANDS *POISED* --UNCERTAIN WHETHER TO *CHARGE* THE THRONE, OR REVERT TO HER *ACT*--

AH! NOW *THIS* IS DECIDEDLY MORE *INTER-ESTING*.

A *WOMAN* WIELDING A *BLADE!*

I'VE NO TASTE FOR VILE *ACRO-BATICS* --BUT A FIGHT *TO THE DEATH* -- NOW *THAT* WOULD TRULY *AMUSE* ME!

IT *MIGHT* EVEN REGALE ME ENOUGH TO GIVE *FIVE GOLD PIECES* TO THE MAN IF HE *SURVIVES*--

--AND *TEN* TO THE *WIFE* IF HE DOES *NOT!*

YOU'LL *NOT* PLAY WITH *OUR* LIVES, STYGIAN!

WORDLESS, PTOR-NUBIS STEPS *FORWARD*, WITH A SURPRISING SPEED--TO *TOUCH* THE SHE-CORSAIR LIGHTLY ON THE *FORE-HEAD*.

:UNNHH--!?:

SHE *STIFFENS* AT HIS TOUCH-- HER WHOLE BODY SEEMS TO *SHUD-DER*--

THEN, WHEN HE STEPS *AWAY*...

HAVE *AT* YOU, NORTHERN DEVIL!

OF A SUDDEN, CONAN SENSES THE *TRUTH* HE SHOULD HAVE GUESSED:

THE DUSKY *PTOR-NUBIS*, WHOM HE HAD THOUGHT BUT AN *EMISSARY*, IS IN TRUTH A *WIZARD* -- SENT NORTH BY THE STYGIAN KING AND HIS SORCEROUS CIRCLE, THE *BLACK RING!*

CONAN HAS *HEARD* OF THESE MEN WHO CAN FORCE ANY TO *OBEY* THEM--

--MERELY BY THE LAYING UPON OF *HANDS*.

NOW, THIS WIZARDRY HAS TURNED BÊLIT INTO A *KILLER*-- WITH NO MORE THOUGHT FOR HER *LOVER* THAN FOR THE COUNTLESS *STYGIANS* SHE'S SENT TO THE BRINY DEEP.

AND, SINCE CONAN IS FIGHTING *DEFENSIVELY*--

--IT IS *SHE* WHO DRAWS *FIRST BLOOD!*

CROM! THIS IS GETTING *SERIOUS!*

STILL BÊLIT'S HYPNOTIC STATE MAKES HER EVER-SO-SLIGHTLY *SLOWER* THAN USUAL--

--GIVING THE BARBARIAN HIS CHANCE TO SNEAK *BELOW* HER ATTACK--

--AND GRASP HER *WRIST* IN AN UNBREAKABLE *VISE!*

WOMAN-- *HEAR* ME!

WE MUST NOT BE *MINDLESS PUPPETS* FOR THESE DOGS! WE--

THE BLANK *STARE* SHE RETURNS TELLS CONAN HE MIGHT AS WELL BE TALKING TO ONE *LONG DEAD*--

THUS, AS THE SHEER *HORROR* OF IT TAKES HIM BACK-- SHE *STRIKES*, IN YET ANOTHER WAY!

ARRR

HALT!

BUT *NIM-KARRAK*... THE BEST IS YET TO *COME*, IF YOU LEAVE THEM BE...!

I SAID *HOLD!* THIS IS STILL *MY* COURT-- *MY* CITY--

THERE WILL BE BLOOD SHED HERE WHEN *I* DECREE IT-- I, AND NO ONE *ELSE!*

AS YOU *WISH*, O KING. AFTER ALL, I AM BUT A HUMBLE *COUNSELLOR*.

COUNSELLOR, *PERHAPS*... BUT HUMBLE, *NEVER*!

CONAN DOES NOT LIKE THE SINISTER GLINT IN THE STYGIAN'S EYES AS HE STALKS OFF, FOLLOWED BY HIS DUSKY ENTOURAGE...

BUT SUDDENLY, MORE IMMEDIATE MATTERS PRESS IT UPON HIM...

YOU ARE *GOOD FIGHTERS*, BOTH OF YOU.

YOU, OUTLANDER--WE CAN USE YOUR SWORD AND ACROBATIC SKILLS IN OUR *ARMY*.

AND AS FOR YOUR *WIFE*--

WELL, A *SOLDIER* HAS PRECIOUS LITTLE NEED OF A *SPOUSE*... THE MORE SO SINCE *MY* SOLDIERS SERVE FOR *TWENTY YEARS*.

AND SO, I WILL TAKE HER FOR *MYSELF*... AT LEAST UNTIL I *TIRE* OF HER.

BY ISHTAR, THERE IS SOMETHING THAT *DRAWS* ME TO THE WENCH!

CONAN--WHAT'S HE *SAYING*? WHAT THE DEVIL *HAPPENED* TO ME? I FEEL SO--

JUST GO *ALONG* WITH HIM, GIRL, AND PLAY IT BY *EAR*.

AND DON'T *KILL* HIM TOO SOON-- OR WE'RE *BOTH* DEAD.

I'LL *COME* TO YOU AS SOON AS I CAN *GET AWAY*.

BUT, THE NEXT MOMENT, IT ABRUPTLY OCCURS TO THE CIMMERIAN THAT THAT MAY TAKE A WHILE...

THIS WAY, BARBARIAN!

AYE! *WE'LL* MAKE A *SOLDIER* OUT OF YOU-- NOT A GRUNTING *SAVAGE*.

CONAN GRITS HIS TEETH-- AND WAITS HIS CHANCE.

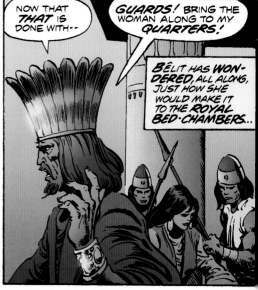

NOW THAT *THAT* IS DONE WITH--

GUARDS! BRING THE WOMAN ALONG TO MY *QUARTERS!*

BÊLIT HAS WONDERED, ALL ALONG, JUST HOW SHE WOULD MAKE IT TO THE ROYAL BED-CHAMBERS...

NOW, THAT TURNS OUT TO BE THE *LEAST* OF HER PROBLEMS...

BY *BEL*, GIRL--YOU LOOK *FAMILIAR*, BLAZING BLACK EYES AND ALL!

HAVE YOU EVER, PERHAPS, BEEN A *DANCING* GIRL IN THE SLAVE BAZAARS OF *ZINGARA*?

I WAS *THERE* THREE YEARS AGO, AND I *RECALL* A GIRL WHO--

YOU'RE WITH A *KING* NOW, NOT SOME SWEATY, STINKING *PEASANT YOKEL*.

NO. *NEVER.*

YOU MEAN... "NEVER, *SIRE*!"

"NEVER, *SIRE*," THEN.

THAT'S *BETTER*. YOU'RE A *SAUCY BAGGAGE*-- BUT, I DARE SAY A FLAGON OF *ARGOSSEAN WINE* WILL COOL YOUR IRE.

IT'S A *GOOD* VINTAGE-- THE YEAR OF THE *RAM*, I THINK...

STRANGE, THOUGH. I HAVE BEEN KING FOR WELL OVER A *DECADE* NOW, YET I'VE *NEVER* BEHELD ANYONE WHO RADIATED *DARK FIRE* SUCH AS YOU DO!

PERHAPS I'LL RADIATE EVEN *MORE*, SIRE... AND *SOON*.

IF YOU *DO*, THERE'LL BE A PLEASANT *SPOT* FOR YOU HERE IN THE PALACE.

TAKE A *CHAIR*, MY DEAR.

I VOW, IT IS *LONELY* WEARING THIS CROWN-- AND I ALWAYS WELCOME A CHANCE TO TAKE IT *OFF*.

THEN YOU *SHOULD* DO SO, SIRE...

AND, MAY *ISHTAR* TAKE YOUR DAMNED SOUL--

19

--MAYBE I'LL SEVER YOUR *HEAD* TO KEEP IT *COMPANY!*

WHAT THE DEVIL--?

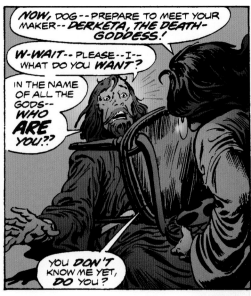

NOW, DOG-- PREPARE TO MEET YOUR MAKER-- *DERKETA, THE DEATH-GODDESS!*

W-WAIT-- PLEASE--I-- WHAT DO YOU *WANT?*

IN THE NAME OF ALL THE GODS-- *WHO ARE YOU??*

YOU *DON'T* KNOW ME YET, *DO* YOU?

WELL, *LOOK DEEP* INTO THESE EYES-- THESE *DARK* EYES, FLASHING WITH UNBRIDLED *HATRED!*

REMEMBER A *CHILD'S* EYES, THAT STARED THUS AT YOU ON A BLOODY NIGHT MORE THAN *TEN YEARS GONE!*

NOW DO YOU KNOW ME, NIM-KARRAK' THE *REGICIDE?*

CHILD? TEN YEA--?

OH *GODS-- GODS!*

BÊLIT!

IT IS *BÊLIT*, DAUGHTER OF *ATRAHASIS--* COME BACK FROM THE *DEAD!*

NOT FROM THE *DEAD*, USURPER-- BUT FROM THE *SOUTHERN ISLES* OFF THE *BLACK COAST!*

--COME BACK TO CLAIM HER *RIGHTFUL REVENGE!*

THEN-- *YOU* ARE THE *SHE-PIRATE* CALLED BÊLIT-- THE ONE THEY CALL THE *QUEEN OF THE BLACK COAST?!*

I KNEW THE *NAME* WAS THE SAME--BUT, I NEVER *DREAMED--*

NO MATTER-- FOR TODAY YOU *DIE*, EVEN AS MY FATHER DIED--

NO-- *WAIT!* YOU ARE *WRONG--!*

YOUR FATHER IS *NOT* DEAD!

HE *LIVES!*

WHAT? IF YOU'RE *LYING*, YOU LILY-LIVERED *PIG*--!

I--I *SWEAR*, GIRL--I TELL THE *TRUTH*, LIKE A MAN ON HIS *DEATH-BED*!

WHICH YOU *ARE*! GO ON.

THE WHOLE PALACE REVOLT WAS THE *STYGIANS'* IDEA--NOT *MINE*--

PTOR-NUBIS WAS SENT NORTH BY *CTESPHON* HIMSELF TO MASTERMIND IT!

HE *SLEW* THE STYGIAN WHO WAS KILLING YOUR SIRE--WISHING TO KEEP YOUR FATHER *ALIVE*, A THREAT OVER *MY* HEAD!

O-OF COURSE, I *MYSELF* WOULD HAVE SPARED ATRA-HASIS, IF I COULD HAVE *REACHED* HIM.

AND WHERE *IS* MY FATHER?

THEY TOOK HIM TO *STYGIA*--TO ITS CAPITAL, *LUXUR*!

YOU'RE TOO *FRIGHTENED* TO LIE--EXCEPT FOR THE *SELF-SERVING* PARTS.

I'LL STILL *KILL* YOU, LIKE THE *CUR* YOU ARE--

BUT I'LL DO IT WITH A *SWORD*, AT LEAST--NOT A JAGGED *BOTTLE.*

YOU'LL *NOT* DO IT AT *ALL*, DAUGHTER OF ATRAHASIS!

PTOR-NUBIS! BUT--THAT DOOR WAS *LOCKED*!

THERE ARE *NO* DOORS WHICH ARE LOCKED TO A SOR-CERER OF THE *BLACK RING*!

NIM-KARRAK IS A *POOR* EXCUSE FOR EVEN A *PUPPET* MONARCH, ADMITTEDLY...

STILL, THE *PEOPLE* WOULD BE DRIVEN TO THE EDGE OF *REBELLION* IF A *STYGIAN* OPENLY ASCEND-ED TO THE THRONE.

OR, IF THEY DID NOT, THE *KOTHIANS* MIGHT DECLARE WAR ON US--TO SAFEGUARD THEIR *OWN* BORDERS.

SO YOU SEE, YOU MUST *NOT* KILL NIM-KARRAK OUT OF *PERSONAL PIQUE.*

COME, MY CHILD--LET ME TAKE YOUR *HAND* AND LEAD YOU GENTLY TO--

ISHTAR! YOU MUST THINK ME A CHILD *INDEED*--

SET!

--TO LET *THAT* BEWITCHED HAND CARESS ME AGAIN!

--BUT I *CAN* TAKE MY *LEAVE!*

CAN'T TAKE MY *SWORD*--

WH--?

LOOK! THE WAY THE WENCH *RUNS*-- SHE MUST BE *FLEEING* OUR *KING!*

GET HER!

WHEN YOU HAVE AN *EAGLE* IN THE *HAND*, DOG--

--BEST NOT TO BOTHER WITH THE *HAWK* IN THE *TREE!*

AAAA

QUICK AS A HILL-PANTHER, CONAN RETRIEVES HIS SWORD--

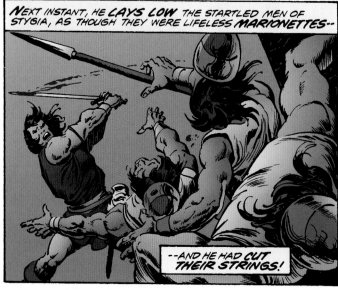

NEXT INSTANT, HE LAYS LOW THE STARTLED MEN OF STYGIA, AS THOUGH THEY WERE LIFELESS MARIONETTES--

--AND HE HAD CUT THEIR STRINGS!

TELL ME-- DID YOU GET WHAT WE CAME FOR?

THE *VIAL?* AYE!

AND DOES THE *TRAITOR* STILL BREATHE?

AYE, CURSE HIM-- BUT, THERE'S *MORE*--!

22

TELL ME ALL ABOUT IT WHEN WE GET BACK TO THE *TIGRESS*, GIRL!

RIGHT NOW, GRAB ONE OF THESE FALLING *BLADES* AND LEND A *HAND*!

GLADLY!

I HOPE THE *MUD'S* TO YOUR LIKING, STYGIAN.

WE'VE NEED OF YOUR *CHARIOT*!

MOMENTS LATER, AFTER A CAREENING *RIDE* THRU THE BROAD, SPACEOUS AVENUES OF *ASGALUN*--

WE'RE IN *LUCK*! THE CITY GATES ARE *OPEN*--

--AND ONLY *TWO MEN* STANDING GUARD!

AS WELL NOT TO HAVE *ANY* GUARDS AT *ALL*!

THEN, WHEN THE PANTING STEEDS HAVE PROPELLED THE CHARIOT FAR ENOUGH FROM THE *CRIES* OF THE CITY...

...AND YOU *BELIEVE* THE *USURPER*, WHEN HE SAYS YOUR *FATHER* WAS SENT *ALIVE*, YEARS AGO, TO *LUXUR*?

I DO.

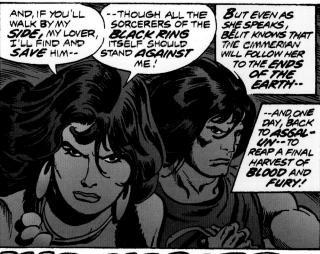

AND, IF YOU'LL WALK BY MY *SIDE*, MY LOVER, I'LL FIND AND *SAVE* HIM--

--THOUGH ALL THE SORCERERS OF THE *BLACK RING* ITSELF SHOULD STAND *AGAINST* ME!

BUT EVEN AS SHE SPEAKS, BÉLIT KNOWS THAT THE CIMMERIAN WILL FOLLOW HER TO THE *ENDS OF THE EARTH*--

--AND, ONE DAY, BACK TO *ASSAL-UN*--TO REAP A FINAL HARVEST OF *BLOOD* AND *FURY*!

NEXT ISSUE: **HE WHO WAITS..** AT THE WELL OF SKELOS!

"Know, O prince, that between the years when the oceans drank Atlantis and the gleaming cities, and the rise of the sons of Aryas, there was an Age undreamed of, when shining kingdoms lay spread across the world like blue mantles beneath the stars.
"Hither came Conan, the Cimmerian, black-haired, sullen-eyed, sword in hand, a thief, a reaver, a slayer, with gigantic melancholies and gigantic mirth, to tread the jeweled thrones of the Earth under his sandaled feet."

— The Nemedian Chronicles.

Stan Lee PRESENTS: CONAN THE BARBARIAN™

HE WHO WAITS -- IN THE WELL OF SKELOS!

THE SLOW, STEADY RHYTHM OF A SINGLE PAIR OF OARS BREAKS THE NIGHTTIME SILENCE SOMEWHERE OFF THE RUGGED COASTS OF SHEM...

...AS CONAN AND BÊLIT DRAW NEAR THE PIRATE SHIP TIGRESS, WHICH LIES AT ANCHOR AT THE APPOINTED PLACE.

NO SENSE IN BROODING, GIRL!

THIS TIME TOMORROW, WE'LL HAVE MAPPED OUT A PLAN TO RESCUE YOUR FATHER FROM THE ACCURSED STYGIANS.

I KNOW WE'LL RESCUE HIM, MY LOVER-- OR ELSE DIE TRYING.

YET, IT'S STILL SUCH A SHOCK TO ME --TO LEARN, AFTER ALL THESE YEARS, THAT HE IS STILL ALIVE--

--A CAPTIVE PAWN IN THE DEADLY GAME THAT NATIONS PLAY!

ROY THOMAS & JOHN BUSCEMA
WRITER/EDITOR   ILLUSTRATOR

ERNIE CHAN, EMBELLISHER

J. COSTANZA letterer

FREELY ADAPTED FROM A PLOT BY ROBERT E. HOWARD CREATOR OF CONAN

SOONER OR LATER, *EVERY* MAN'S A PAWN IN *SOMEONE'S* GAME...

...EVEN ONE WHO WAS A *KING,* LIKE YOUR *FATHER.*

THERE'S THE *BOARD-ING-ROPE.*

AYE-- BUT, I DIDN'T *SEE* OR *HEAR* ANYONE TOSS IT *OVER.*

BY CROM, YOU'RE *RIGHT!* IT'S NOT *LIKE* M'GORA TO LET YOUR CORSAIRS *SLACK OFF.*

A *RAIDING-CREW* COULD HAVE BOARDED THE SHIP AS EASILY AS *WE.*

I TELL YOU, CONAN, *HEADS* WILL ROLL, WHEN I FIND THE MAN WHO--

YOU NEED LOOK *NO FURTHER* FOR HIM, WHITE WITCH, THAN OVER YOUR OWN PALE *SHOULDER!*

WHAT? WHO THE *DEVIL*--?

YOU CAN *GUESS* THE ANSWER TO *THAT* ONE, WOMAN.

KAWAKU! WHAT ARE YOU AND THOSE OTHERS DOING *SKULKING ABOUT* LIKE SHADOWS-- POINTING SPEARS--?

YOU *KNOW* WHAT IT MEANS-- SO DO NOT ACT THE *FOOL!*

THESE ARE NO LONGER *YOUR* BLACK CORSAIRS; THEY OBEY *KAWAKU* NOW!

ARE THEY *DOGS*-- TO FOLLOW A SPINELESS *JACKAL* LIKE YOU?

BESIDES, THIS ISN'T *ALL* MY CREW-- JUST A *HANDFUL* OF THEM --

--AND THE *WORST* OF THE LOT, TO *BOOT.*

M'GORA AND THE OTHERS ARE LOCKED UP IN THE *HOLD...*

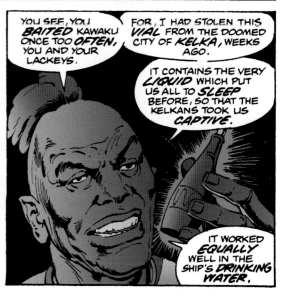

YOU SEE, YOU *BAITED* KAWAKU ONCE TOO *OFTEN,* YOU AND YOUR LACKEYS.

FOR, I HAD STOLEN THIS *VIAL* FROM THE DOOMED CITY OF *KELKA,* WEEKS AGO.

IT CONTAINS THE VERY *LIQUID* WHICH PUT US ALL TO *SLEEP* BEFORE, SO THAT THE KELKANS TOOK US *CAPTIVE.*

IT WORKED *EQUALLY* WELL IN THE SHIP'S *DRINKING WATER.*

NOW, CHAMA-- TAKE THEM BELOW WITH THE OTHERS, AND--

A-AYE, KAWAKU THEY-- A'EEEE!

YOU BACK-STAB-BING DOG!

YOU'LL GO BELOW ALL RIGHT--

--AND GIVE MY REGARDS TO THE SHARKS!

BÊLIT'S SAVAGE CORSAIRS BELIEVE HER TO BE A DEATH-GODDESS, AND HER BARBARIAN MATE TO BE AMRA, LORD OF LIONS...

THUS, THEY REACT A BIT TOO SLOWLY WHEN THEIR TWO CAPTIVES SUDDENLY LASH OUT--

AND, THE FEAR THEY HAVE ALWAYS FELT FOR THESE TWO, WHO SEEM AS MUCH LIKE DEMONS AS GODS, RISES ANEW--

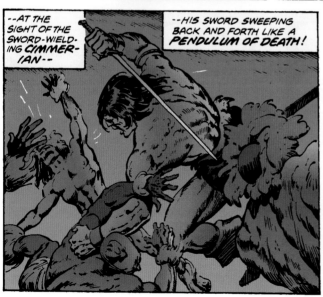

--AT THE SIGHT OF THE SWORD-WIELDING CIMMER-IAN--

--HIS SWORD SWEEPING BACK AND FORTH LIKE A PENDULUM OF DEATH!

BUT KAWAKU, FOR ALL HIS COWARDICE, KNOWS ALL IS LOST UNLESS HE HIMSELF TAKES PRE-CIPITATE ACTION...

SO HE DOES!

YOU CRAVEN *HYENAS!* YOU'LL *PAY* FOR THAT BLOW!

COME IN *CLOSER,* AND HEAR MY *SONG OF STEEL!*

NO *NEED* TO DO THAT--

WHEN MY *SPEAR,* HURLED FROM THIS DISTANCE, CAN SLAY YOU *WITHOUT* RISK!

HOLD, AWOGMU-- YOU *FORGET* WHY YOU MEN WERE WON OVER TO MUTINY IN THE *FIRST* PLACE!

I CAN GUESS, THOUGH.

AYE, "GODDESS"-- IT'S YOUR *LOOT* WE WANT!

ALMOST EVERY *COIN* OR *JEWEL* WE'VE PIRATED THESE PAST YEARS HAS BEEN BURIED BY YOU, ON A *NAMELESS ISLE* NOT FAR FROM HERE.

WITH GOOD *REASON* IT SEEMS.

BUT, ONLY *M'GORA* AND A FEW OTHERS --AND *AMRA*** -- HAVE BEEN ALLOWED TO *ACCOMPANY* YOU TO THE SITE.

*** CONAN IS KNOWN AS *AMRA* ON ON THE BLACK COAST. --ROY

WE *MAY* SPARE YOU, IF YOU WILL *SHOW* US TO THE SPOT WHERE THE *TREASURE* IS BURIED, SO THAT-- ⸗*AAARRH--!*⸗

AND HOW WILL YOU BE ABLE TO *SEE* IT, DOG--

--WITH MY *SPITTLE* IN YOUR EYE?

YOU *WITCH!*

YOU'LL *NOT* SPIT ON *ME* AND LIVE TO LAUGH ABOUT IT!

BY DAGON, I'LL RUN YOU THRU *MYSELF* --AND TORTURE *M'GORA* TILL HE TALKS OR DIES!

WAIT!

KAWAKU! AMRA IS *AWAKE!* HIS SKULL MUST BE *THICK.*

VERY THICK-- NOT TO HAVE *SORTED OUT* THE VIPERS IN OUR MIDST, *MONTHS* AGO!

I *HEARD* YOU, KAWAKU--

--AND *I'LL* LEAD YOU TO THE TREASURE--BUT ONLY IF YOU *SPARE BÊLIT!*

WHAT?? THAT'S **MY** TREASURE, BARBARIAN-- STORED AGAINST THE DAY WHEN IT WOULD PAY AN **ARMY** TO MARCH AGAINST **ASGALUN!**

YOU'VE **NO RIGHT** TO GIVE IT OVER TO THESE MUTINOUS SWINE-- NOT EVEN TO **SAVE MY LIFE!**

NO RIGHT!

BUT, CONAN IS GRIMLY **SILENT.**

YOU **SEE,** "GODDESS"? **AMRA** IS ACTING FAR **WISER** THAN YOU.

TIE HER TO THE **MAST--** AND WE'LL BE **OFF.**

WAIT--!

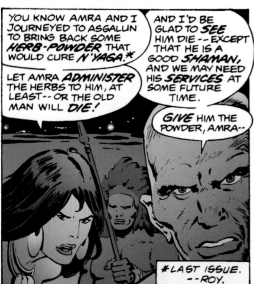

YOU KNOW AMRA AND I JOURNEYED TO ASGALUN TO BRING BACK SOME **HERB-POWDER** THAT WOULD CURE **N'YAGA.***

LET AMRA **ADMINISTER** THE HERBS TO HIM, AT LEAST-- OR THE OLD MAN WILL **DIE!**

AND I'D BE GLAD TO **SEE** HIM DIE-- EXCEPT THAT HE IS A GOOD **SHAMAN,** AND WE MAY NEED HIS **SERVICES** AT SOME FUTURE TIME.

GIVE HIM THE POWDER, AMRA--

*LAST ISSUE. --ROY.

--WHILE YOU EBON LANDLUBBERS **CAST OFF!**

WE'RE BOUND FOR THE **ISLE OF HIDDEN GOLD!**

AWOGMU-- BRING UP THE **OTHER** CAPTIVES, TO BRING HER **ABOUT!**

HEAR ME, YOU WHO WOULD REMAIN **LOYAL** TO A **HELPLESS WHITE WOMAN--**

SHE **LIVES--** BUT ONLY SO LONG AS YOU OBEY **KAWAKU.**

TWO MEN WILL GUARD HER AT ALL TIMES-- AND **SLAY** HER, IF ANY BUT RAISE A **HAND** TO ME.

HEAR ME, MY CORSAIRS!

I'LL ASK **NO MAN** TO SERVE A COWARDLY **DOG** LIKE KAWAKU.

WELL? WILL YOU SWEAR TO **SERVE** ME NOW?

FORGET ME-- AND **STRIKE** NOW, FOR YOUR OWN **FREEDOM!**

28

M'GORA AND THE OTHERS LOOK AT THEIR *SHE-PIRATE CAPTAIN*-- THEN AT THE TALL BRONZED *OUTLANDER* WHO IS HER RIGHT HAND.

WITHOUT A WORD, HE SHAKES HIS *HEAD*...AND GESTURES THEM TO GET TO *WORK*.

AND, *ALSO* WITHOUT A WORD...

...THEY *OBEY*.

FOR THE FIRST TIME, BÊLIT REALIZES THAT THESE MEN NOW OBEY *CONAN* AS READILY AS *HERSELF*...

...AND SHE FEELS THE *LOSS OF POWER,* LIKE A BLOW TO THE HEAD.

NOW, HEEDLESS AS A GYPSY WIND, THE *TIGRESS* SAILS AS IF TO SAIL TO THE END OF THE *WESTERN OCEAN* ITSELF.

NO ISLAND SHOWS HERE ON HYBORIAN MAPS-- YET WITHIN A FEW SHORT DAYS...

LAND HO!

TRUSTING *NO ONE* SINCE HE HIMSELF CAN BE TRUSTED BY NONE, *KAWAKU* HIMSELF ACCOMPANIES THE *LANDING PARTY* ON THE JUNGLE-COVERED ISLE...

MAKE NO *FALSE MOVE* WHILE WE ARE ASHORE, WHITE SCUM...

...OR ELSE YOU *KNOW* WHAT WILL HAPPEN TO YOUR *WOMAN!*

CONAN SAYS NOTHING... FOR, WHAT HAS A *LION* TO DO WITH A *JACKAL*?

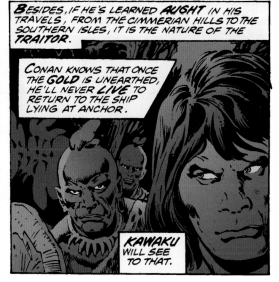

BESIDES, IF HE'S LEARNED *AUGHT* IN HIS TRAVELS, FROM THE CIMMERIAN HILLS TO THE SOUTHERN ISLES, IT IS THE NATURE OF THE *TRAITOR*.

CONAN KNOWS THAT ONCE THE *GOLD* IS UNEARTHED, HE'LL NEVER *LIVE* TO RETURN TO THE SHIP LYING AT ANCHOR.

KAWAKU WILL SEE TO THAT.

BUT MEANWHILE, HE LEADS THEM *ON*... THRU THE CLEFT BOLE OF A GARGANTUAN *TREE* THAT TOWERS TO THE HEAVENS LIKE *YIGG*, THE TREE OF *LIFE*...

...FAR *PAST* THE POINT WHERE ANY SAVE HIMSELF, M'GORA, AND A FEW CHOSEN *OTHERS* WERE EVER PERMITTED TO *ACCOMPANY* BÊLIT.

TILL, AT LAST, IN A RUBBLE-STREWN *CLEARING*, THEY BEHOLD--

THE TEMPLE OF THE *TOAD!*

MANHOOD OF *AJUJO!* SHE *DARED* TO BURY TREASURE IN *SUCH A PLACE!?*

SO *BÊLIT* CHRISTENED IT-- THOUGH WE'VE NO IDEA WHAT *NAMELESS HANDS* REARED IT, IN AGES PAST.

WHAT *BETTER* PLACE TO KEEP *FAINT-HEARTED FOOLS* AWAY FROM IT?

YOU *SEE*, KAWAKU? YOUR LACKEYS ARE *FRIGHTENED* TO GO IN.

SO, WE KNEW, MIGHT *OTHERS* BE.

WE MUST *GO BACK*, KAWAKU!

ONLY *DEMONS* DWELL IN ABODES LIKE THIS!

≡*PHAGH!*≡ YOU ARE ALL *DOLTS* AND OLD, WIZENED *WOMEN!*

LEAD THE *WAY*, AMRA--AND MY *SPEAR* FOR THE BACK OF ANY WHO WOULD *TURN AWAY!*

AS YOU *WISH.*

KAWAKU'S WORDS ARE UNACCUSTOMEDLY *BRAVE*...

YET, IT PROVES MERE *BRAVADO* AS THEY PASS THRU THE GREAT STONE *PORTALS* WHICH SERVE AS THE YAWNING *MOUTH* OF THE TOAD-IDOL...

...AND THE *SHADOWS* SEEM TO CLOSE AROUND THEM, DEVOURING THE LIGHT AS IF IT WERE *FOOD.*

WITHIN, THEY PASS WITH SOFTLY-ECHOING STEP OVER A GREAT, WORN *STONE...*

...MARKED WITH A *TONGUE* EVEN THE *NEMEDIAN SCHOLARS* WOULD TAKE *DECADES* TO *DECIPHER...*

...TO STAND AT LAST IN THE *CENTER* OF THE VAST, *TIME-RUINED* TEMPLE:

WE LOWERED THE BOOTY DOWN INTO THIS *WELL*--WHICH BÊLIT BELIEVES TO BE THE FABLED *WELL OF SKELOS.*

DOWN THERE, KAWAKU.

THERE IS A SWIFT, INVOLUNTARY *INTAKE OF BREATH* FROM KAWAKU AND HIS WIDE-EYED MEN.

FOR, EVEN *THEY* HAVE HEARD OF *SKELOS,* ANCIENT MAGE AND AUTHOR OF *SORCEROUS SCROLLS...*

AND THE *WELL OF SKELOS,* WHERE DEMONS GUARD HIS *LONG-DEAD BONES,* IS A PART OF *BLACK COAST* LORE AS WELL AS *STYGIAN* AND *HYBORIAN.*

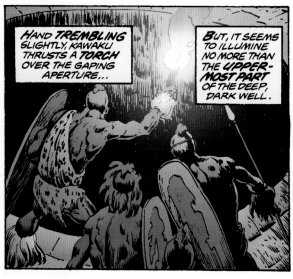

HAND *TREMBLING* SLIGHTLY, KAWAKU THRUSTS A *TORCH* OVER THE GAPING APERTURE...

BUT, IT SEEMS TO *ILLUMINE* NO MORE THAN THE *UPPER-MOST PART* OF THE DEEP, DARK WELL.

CONAN CAN *SENSE* THE ALMOST PALPABLE *INNER STRUGGLINGS* OF THE MUTINEER:

THE SPECTRE OF *FEAR,* GRAPPLING TALON-TO-THROAT WITH THE GREY GOBLIN OF *GREED.*

STILL, CAN THERE BE ANY *DOUBT*--

--THAT CANCEROUS **GREED** WILL WIN OUT AGAINST FEARS ONLY **HALF-FORMED**?

WELL? WE HAVE **ROPE.** WHICH OF YOU WILL BE **LOWERED** INTO THE WELL, TO SEE IF AMRA **LIES**?

THE MEN ARE **SILENT**, THEIR JAWS SET.

KAWAKU KNOWS THAT THEY HAVE BEEN **PUSHED** TO THEIR LIMIT--FIRST IN OVER-THROWING A **GODDESS ON EARTH**, NOW IN CHALLENGING **DEVILS** AS WELL.

IF HE PUSHES THEM **FURTHER**, THEY WILL TURN THEIR **SPEARS** ON HIM, OUT OF SHEER **FRIGHT.** THUS--

I WILL GO MYSELF.

I, KAWAKU!

UNSPEAKING, THE MEN **LOWER** THEIR TORCH-WIELDING LEADER.

AND, IF KAWAKU HAS ANY LAST-MINUTE **REGRETS**, HE DOES NOT DARE **VOICE** THEM.

AT LEAST HIS **BACKSIDE** IS SAFE-- WITH A **TRIO OF SHAFTS** POINTED AT THE WHITE BARBARIAN'S NECK.

HOW KAWAKU WOULD LOVE TO GIVE THE ORDER TO **PIERCE** THOSE CORDED MUSCLES, ERE HE **DESCENDS** INTO HELLISH BLACKNESS.

BUT, HE MAY YET BE **NEEDED** IN SOME WAY, JUST A LITTLE WHILE LONGER...

...SO THE USURPER **CONTENTS** HIMSELF WITH:

TILL WE **MEET AGAIN,** AMRA.

GOOD-BYE, KAWAKU.

THE DIFFERENCE IN PHRASING IS **LOST** ON THE CORSAIR...

...AS HE IS LOWERED INTO A DARKNESS WHICH ONLY **SEEMS** TO RECEDE BEFORE HIS WAVERING TORCH...

...YET **ENGULFS** HIM, NAY, SEEMS ALMOST TO **SWALLOW** HIM **WHOLE**...

...TILL ONLY THE BAREST FLAME OF THE **TORCH** ITSELF IS SEEN.

THEN, **IT TOO** IS GONE FROM SIGHT.

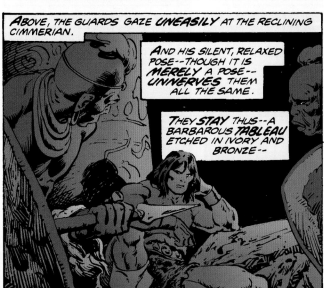

ABOVE, THE GUARDS GAZE **UNEASILY** AT THE RECLINING CIMMERIAN.

AND HIS SILENT, RELAXED POSE--THOUGH IT IS **MERELY** A POSE-- **UNNERVES** THEM ALL THE SAME.

THEY **STAY** THUS--A BARBAROUS **TABLEAU** ETCHED IN IVORY AND BRONZE--

--TILL ABRUPTLY, **WITHOUT WARNING**--!

KAWAKU!

HE **SCREAMS**-- FROM DEEP IN THE **WELL**!

LOOK! THE **ROPE**-- IT HAS GONE **SLACK**!

THEN, EITHER HE HAS **FALLEN**-- OR ELSE HE HAS REACHED THE **BOTTOM**!

BUT, THAT **SHRIEK**--!

THERE IS NO ANSWER.

KAWAKU!

WAIT! FEEL!

THE ROPE IS **TAUT** AGAIN! HE HAS **HOLD** OF IT.

AND--THE **WEIGHT**-- IT IS **MORE** THAN BEFORE!

33

FOOLS! IT IS BECAUSE HE IS BRINGING BACK SOME OF THE *TREASURE*!

PULL!

BUT-- WHY DID HE NOT *ANSWER* YOUR CALL, AWOGMU?

WHAT DOES IT *MATTER*? JUST *KEEP* PULLING!

LOOK! WE HAVE REELED IN ALMOST THE *WHOLE LENGTH* OF ROPE.

I HEAR HIS *FEET*, SCUFFLING AGAINST THE *SIDES* OF THE WELL.

HERE, KAWAKU-- LET ME *RELIEVE* YOU OF YOUR GOLDEN *BURDEN*!

TAKE MY *HAND*, SO THAT--

NO! NNNOOO--!

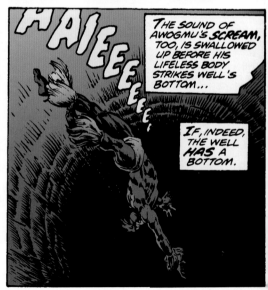

HAIEEEEEE!

THE SOUND OF AWOGMU'S *SCREAM*, TOO, IS SWALLOWED UP BEFORE HIS LIFELESS BODY STRIKES WELL'S BOTTOM...

IF, INDEED, THE WELL *HAS* A BOTTOM.

AND THEN, SUDDENLY, A *MONSTROUS THING OF NIGHTMARE* SHAMBLES FORTH, DRIPPING SLIME AND SLAVERING....!

NO LONGER DO THE TERROR-STRICKEN CORSAIRS *DOUBT* WHAT HAS HAPPENED TO *KAWAKU*...

GUH-RUNK!

IN FACT, NO LONGER DO THEY EVEN THINK OF HIM...

NOR DO THE THREE GUARDS REMEMBER ANY MORE HIS COMMAND NOT TO TURN THEIR BACKS ON AMRA.

THEY WERE WISE WORDS, FOR ALL THAT THEY WERE UTTERED BY A DEAD COWARD.

ARRRH

MEANWHILE, THE CREATURE'S HIDEOUS, FROGLIKE *GRUNTING* ECHOES INSTANTLY THRU THE TEMPLE--

GRONK!

--AS THE SCENE WITHIN BECOMES ONE OF *SLAUGHTER*, NOT MERELY OF *SLAYING*.

STILL, THE *CORSAIRS* RECRUITED BY BÊLIT ARE MOSTLY *NOT* COWARDS--

AND, THOUGH FRIGHTENED OF THE SUPERNATURAL, SEVERAL OF THEM *STAND THEIR GROUND*--

--TO TOSS *INEFFECTUAL SPEARS* AGAINST A THICK LEATHERN *HIDE*--

RHNGK?

--AND *DIE* FOR THEIR COURAGE!

GA-RO-YK!

SO THAT WHEN THEY *DO* FLEE AT LAST--

--IT IS NOT AS *COWARDS*, BUT AS MEN *OVERWHELMED* BY AN *INHUMAN, MURDEROUS FOE!*

AND NOW, THE TOAD-THING LOOKS ABOUT FOR *NEW* MEN TO KILL, TO AVENGE THE *DISTURBING* OF ITS NIGHT-DARK PLACE OF REST--

GUR-GORK

--AND ITS GREAT ROUND EYES FALL ON ONE WHOSE *MAN-SCENT* IS VAGUELY *FAMILIAR* TO IT.

YES, THE *PALE* MANLING HAS BEEN *BEFORE* IN THIS TEMPLE.

FITTING, THEN, THAT THIS TIME HE *STAY HERE*-- FOREVER!

THE *MANLING*, HOWEVER, HAS *OTHER* IDEAS-- AND *GREATER STRENGTH* THAN THE OTHERS!

GORNK!?

THE *TOAD-THING* SENSES *FEAR* IN THE BRONZED ONE-- AS GREAT A FEAR, ALMOST, AS THE *OTHERS* FELT.

YET, CORNERED, HE DOES NOT *GIVE WAY* TO THAT FEAR AS *THEY* DID--

--BUT *FIGHTS BACK*, WITH A BERSERKER FURY WHICH IT HAS NEVER *ENCOUNTERED!*

STILL, IT IS A WILDLY *UNEVEN* BATTLE--*MORTAL MAN* AGAINST *IMMORTAL MONSTER*--

AND *CONAN* KNOWS, AT ONCE, THAT HE MUST *LOSE* IN THE END--

--THAT HE IS BEING *FORCED BACK* TOWARD THE GAPING *WELL OF SKELOS*--

--WHERE *HIS* BODY WILL IN MOMENTS LIE AS LIFELESS AS THOSE OF *KAWAKU* AND *AWOGMU*, UNLESS--

WITH A RESOLVE BORDERING ON *MADNESS*, THE STRAINING BARBARIAN SUDDENLY *STEPS OFF* THE WELL'S EDGE--

GUH-*RONK!*

--AND THE *TOAD-THING*, WHICH WAS NEVER MEANT TRULY TO STAND UPRIGHT, IS CAUGHT *OFF BALANCE--*

--SO THAT IT HURTLES *PAST* HIM IN ITS WANTON *RUSH--*

--TO TOPPLE *BACK* INTO THE STYGIAN *BLACKNESS* WHEN IT CAME!

AS FOR *CONAN:*

ONE WILDLY-FLAILING *HAND* HAS GRASPED THE *SLIPPERY EDGE* OF THE WELL -- GAINING HIM A FEW PRECIOUS MOMENTS OF *LIFE!*

BUT ALREADY HE CAN FEEL HIS FINGERS *SLIDING* SLOWLY TOWARD INEVITABLE *DOOM...*

AND HE KNOWS HE CANNOT *HOLD OUT* FOR LONG, ERE HE *JOINS* THE MONSTER AT WELL'S BOTTOM, TO LEARN IF IT BE *DEAD* OR *ALIVE.*

OTHER MEN WOULD GO TO THEIR DEATHS *CURSING* THE GODS THAT MADE THEM--THEIR *FINAL SCREAM* A HIDEOUS, OBSCENE *BLASPHEMY* AGAINST GODS AND MEN.

CONAN MERELY *GRITS HIS TEETH* -- AND DIGS HIS NAILS *DEEPER,* AS IF TO BITE INTO THE UNYIELDING *STONE* ABOVE.

AND ALL THE WHILE, HE FEELS THOSE NAILS *SLIDE* SOME MORE.

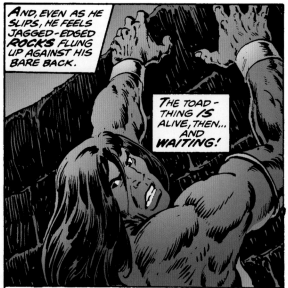

AND, EVEN AS HE SLIPS, HE FEELS JAGGED-EDGED ROCKS FLUNG UP AGAINST HIS BARE BACK.

THE TOAD-THING *IS* ALIVE, THEN... AND *WAITING!*

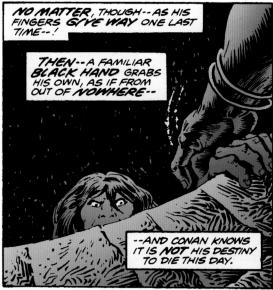

NO MATTER, THOUGH--AS HIS FINGERS *GIVE WAY* ONE LAST TIME--!

THEN--A FAMILIAR *BLACK HAND* GRABS HIS OWN, AS IF FROM OUT OF *NOWHERE*--

--AND CONAN KNOWS IT IS *NOT* HIS DESTINY TO DIE THIS DAY.

M'GORA--LARANGA--AND *BÊLIT!*

YOU'RE *HERE!*

AND LUCKY FOR *YOU* THAT WE CAME WHEN WE *DID*, AMRA!

NO QUARREL *THERE*...

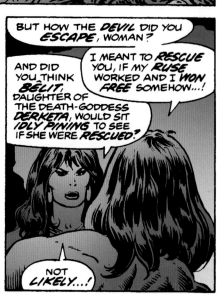

BUT HOW THE *DEVIL* DID YOU *ESCAPE*, WOMAN?

AND DID *YOU* THINK *BÊLIT*, DAUGHTER OF THE DEATH-GODDESS *DERKETA*, WOULD SIT *IDLY PINING* TO SEE IF SHE WERE *RESCUED?*

I MEANT TO *RESCUE* YOU, IF MY *RUSE* WORKED AND I *WON FREE* SOMEHOW...!

NOT *LIKELY*...!

WITH *KAWAKU* AND HIS OTHER LACKEYS GONE, THE *TWO DOGS* HE HAD LEFT TO GUARD ME GREW MORE INTERESTED IN *SWAPPING LIES* THAN IN GUARDING ME.

"MY NAILS ARE AS SHARP AS A LEOPARD'S...

"...WEARING THRU THOSE SLENDER BONDS ERE LONG.

"AND *WHAT MAN*, AYE, EVEN OF THE FIERCE *BLACK CORSAIRS*--

"--CAN STAND IN SPEAR-BATTLE AGAINST *BÊLIT?*"

NOT *MANY,* IT SEEMS.

THEN, I GUESS WE *RETURN* NOW TO THE *TIGRESS?*

NOT *QUITE* YET.

M'GORA?

YES, GODDESS...

YASUNGA! AJONGA!

BRING THE *JEWEL-CHEST* WE WANT TO STORE!

WE *COME,* M'GORA.

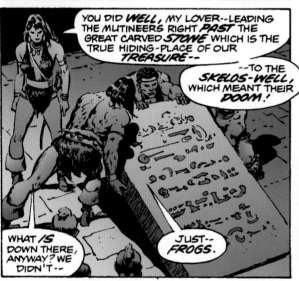

YOU DID *WELL,* MY LOVER-- LEADING THE MUTINEERS RIGHT *PAST* THE GREAT CARVED *STONE* WHICH IS THE TRUE HIDING-PLACE OF OUR *TREASURE*--

--TO THE *SKELOS-WELL,* WHICH MEANT THEIR *DOOM!*

WHAT *IS* DOWN THERE, ANYWAY? WE DIDN'T --

JUST-- *FROGS.*

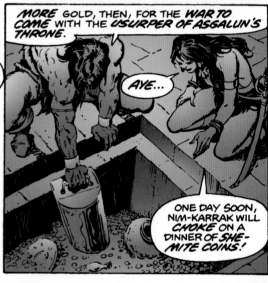

MORE GOLD, THEN, FOR THE *WAR TO COME* WITH THE *USURPER OF ASGALUN'S THRONE.*

AYE...

ONE DAY SOON, NIM-KARRAK WILL *CHOKE* ON A DINNER OF *SHEMITE* COINS!

WHAT OF THOSE WHO *FLED* INTO THE JUNGLE?

LET THEM *DIE* THERE-- FOR, WE KNOW THIS ISLE'S FRUIT IS *VENOMOUS,* ITS WELL- WATER *POISON.*

WE'LL BE *SHORT- HANDED,* PERHAPS...

BUT, BÊLIT'S *NEXT* MISSION IS ONE SHE MUST PURSUE WITH *NO ONE* AT HER SIDE.

NO ONE, YOU MEAN, BUT *CONAN,* ALSO CALLED *AMRA.*

YOU ARE A *PART* OF ME-- AS MUCH AS MY OWN *SWORD.*

MY OWN SHARP, *THIRSTING* SWORD!

NEXT ISSUE: **THE BLACK WALLS** of **KHEMI!**

40

"Know, O prince, that between the years when the oceans drank Atlantis and the gleaming cities, and the rise of the sons of Aryas, there was an Age undreamed of, when shining kingdoms lay spread across the world like blue mantles beneath the stars.

"Hither came Conan, the Cimmerian, black-haired, sullen-eyed, sword in hand, a thief, a reaver, a slayer, with gigantic melancholies and gigantic mirth, to tread the jeweled thrones of the Earth under his sandaled feet."

—*The Nemedian Chronicles.*

STAN LEE PRESENTS: CONAN THE BARBARIAN™

THE BATTLE AT THE BLACK WALLS!

ROY THOMAS WRITER & EDITOR * JOHN BUSCEMA & ERNIE CHAN ARTISTS * JOE ROSEN LETTERER

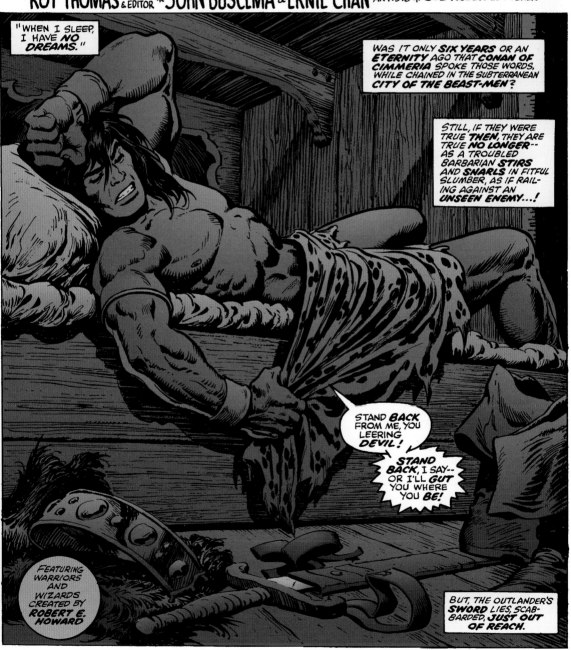

"WHEN I SLEEP, I HAVE *NO DREAMS.*"

WAS IT ONLY *SIX YEARS* OR AN *ETERNITY* AGO THAT *CONAN OF CIMMERIA* SPOKE THOSE WORDS, WHILE CHAINED IN THE SUBTERRANEAN *CITY OF THE BEAST-MEN?*

STILL, IF THEY WERE TRUE *THEN,* THEY ARE TRUE *NO LONGER*-- AS A TROUBLED BARBARIAN *STIRS* AND *SNARLS* IN FITFUL SLUMBER, AS IF RAILING AGAINST AN *UNSEEN ENEMY...!*

STAND *BACK* FROM ME, YOU LEERING *DEVIL!*

STAND *BACK,* I SAY-- OR I'LL *GUT* YOU WHERE YOU *BE!*

FEATURING *WARRIORS* AND *WIZARDS* CREATED BY *ROBERT E. HOWARD*

BUT, THE OUTLANDER'S *SWORD* LIES, SCAB-BARDED, *JUST OUT OF REACH.*

YET, LET US JOURNEY NOW *BEYOND* THE WALL OF SLEEP-- THRU THAT YAWNING *GATE OF IVORY* WHERE THE MIND WANDERS LOST IN THE *HOURS BEFORE WAKING.*

THERE, SURELY ENOUGH, CONAN IS THE *WARRIOR AT BAY* -- HIS BLADE AT THE READY, HIMSELF POISED LIKE A *PANTHER* --

EVEN *CTESPHON, KING OF STYGIA,* DOES NOT LIGHTLY COMMAND *THOTH-AMON OF THE BLACK RING* -- LET ALONE SHALL A *WITLESS BARBARIAN!*

IN *OTHER* TIMES, I WOULD PAY YOU *NO MIND* -- OR ELSE *CRUSH* YOU UNDERFOOT AS CARELESSLY AS I WOULD A *SPIDER.*

BUT, THESE ARE *NOT* OTHER TIMES -- AND SO, I HAVE SUMMONED YOU THROUGH THE PORTALS OF DREAM TO *WARN* YOU --

-- AND THUS, PERHAPS, TO *SPARE* YOUR WORTHLESS LIFE !

THOTH-AMON!

--THOUGH AGAINST A *DISEMBODIED FOE* WHO WEARS THE CURVED HORNS OF A *STYGIAN RAM,* AND WHOSE DARK EYES BURN WITH *FIRES STOKED IN HELL--!*

I *KNOW* YOU-- FOR, THOUGH WE'VE NEVER TRULY MET, OUR *PATHS* HAVE CROSSED SINCE I ROAMED SOUTH INTO THE *HYBORIAN LANDS!*

IN *NUMALIA,* SECOND CITY OF *NEMEDIA,* I SAW YOU-- AFTER I CUT DOWN THE *MAN-HEADED SERPENT* THAT SLEW AT YOUR DISTANT CALL--

--ALSO IN THE *HILLS OF ARGOS,* WHEN I FOUGHT ALONGSIDE *BÊLIT* AND *RED SONJA* AND THE MAN-LEGEND *KING KULL!*

WHY HAVE YOU *BROUGHT* ME TO THIS DISMAL PLACE? *WHY?*

ANSWER ME! I COMMAND YOU!!

SPARE ME!? WELL, SINCE THIS *IS* MERELY A DREAM--

TELL ME WHAT IT *REQUIRES* NOT TO INCUR THE WRATH OF THE FABLED *THOTH-AMON!*

MY DEMANDS ARE *SIMPLE*, BARBARIAN...

SIMPLY *ABANDON* YOUR FUTILE QUEST FOR THE *CAPTIVE KING-FATHER* OF THE SHEMITISH SHE-DEVIL *BÊLIT!*

AND IF *SHE* DOESN'T WANT TO ABANDON THE SEARCH?

DESERT HER! THE WOMAN IS *NOTHING* TO YOU!

AYE-- BUT ONLY BECAUSE YOUR *OTHER* CHOICE WAS TO *WALK THE PLANK!*

SHE IS MY *MATE!*

BUT, WHY SHOULD I PLY YOU WITH *WORDS*-- WHEN A SINGLE *VISION* WOULD BETTER STATE MY CASE?

THE TIGRESS-- BURNING AT SEA!?

AND SO *SHALL* YOUR SHIP, UN-LESS YOU *HEED* MY DEMANDS!

BUT, WHO IS *ON BOARD* HER THEN? OR IS IT JUST A *GHOST SHIP* THAT BURNS?

I HAVE REVEALED ALL I *SHALL*, TO ONE WHOSE *BRAIN* IS TOO SMALL TO *COMPREHEND* MORE...

NOW, WILL YOU DO MY *BIDDING*, AND PERHAPS EVEN LIVE TO BECOME A *GREAT KING*, OR--?

HERE'S MY ANSWER, DOG OF STYGIA!

A SLIVER OF *HYRKANIAN STEEL*, RIGHT BETWEEN THE--

--EYES?

WHERE HAVE YOU *GONE*, YOU SOUTHERN DEMON?

AND-- WHAT *NEW MADNESS* HAVE YOU SENT TO *PLAGUE* ME?

THIS TIME, HOWEVER, IT IS NOT *STYGIAN ACCENTS* WHICH RESPOND...

NOW, AT LAST, THE SHIFTING SEA OF FACES SINGS A DIFFERENT TUNE-- THOUGH HARDLY A SWEETER ONE--

ABANDON THE WOMAN CALLED BÊLIT-- OR WOULD YOU DOOM US ALL?

HAVE YOU NOT ALREADY DONE ENOUGH??

WHAT? WHAT HAVE I DONE, DAMN YOU?

WHAT??

BUT NOW, THERE IS NO ANSWER AT ALL...THE MULTITUDE OF HEADS FADE, AS THOTH-AMON DID BEFORE THEM...

AND CONAN FEELS EVEN HIMSELF FADING, AS IF HE WERE NO MORE REAL THAN THEY...

...ONLY TO WAKE ABRUPTLY, SWEATING, ON BOARD THE GENT TOSSING TIGRESS.

THEN-- IT WAS A DREAM, AFTER ALL!?

CROM TAKE ME, I'D BEGUN TO DOUBT WHETHER IT WAS REAL--OR I WAS!

BÊLIT-- DID YOU--?

BÊLIT...?

BUT, CONAN IS ALONE.

MORE ALONE, PERHAPS, THAN HE HAS EVER BEEN BEFORE.

THUS, SWIFTLY AND WORDLESSLY DONNING HIS LOINCLOTH...

...HE STALKS FORTH TO FACE THE WORLD...

...ONLY A SHADOW OF DOUBT REMAINING THAT IT IS STILL THERE.

BUT, LIKE MANY **BEFORE** HIM, CONAN SWIFTLY DISCOVERS THAT THE WORLD **IS** THERE, CURIOUSLY **INDIFFERENT** TO HIS MORBID INSIGHTS.

THEN, THE UN-ACCUSTOMED MOOD **PASSES,** AS NIGHTMARES **DO** PASS...

...AS HE BEHOLDS HIS RAVEN-TRESSED **PART-NER IN PLUNDER,** SO LOST IN THOUGHT THAT SHE IS **UNAWARE** OF HIS APPROACH...

...UNTIL...

OH-- **CONAN--** I DIDN'T--

I **KNOW.**

AND SUDDENLY, FOR A **FEW SHORT MOMENTS...**

...SHE IS **NO LONGER** THE SELF-STYLED **QUEEN OF THE BLACK COAST,** FEARED FROM ZINGARA TO KUSH...

...BUT ONLY A **WOMAN,** IN NEED OF A **SHOULDER** TO LEAN ON.

I...HAD A **DREAM,** MY LOVER...

"...A DREAM OF **HOW IT WAS** WHEN I WAS A LITTLE GIRL, GROWING UP IN THE PALACE AT **ASGALUN,** PROUD CITY OF **SHEM.**

"I SAW AGAIN MY ROYAL FATHER **ATRAHASIS,** WHO LOVED ME **WONDROUSLY,** IF NOT **WISELY...**

"AND I WITNESSED AGAIN THE **PALACE REVOLT,** LED BY HIS BROTHER **NIM-KARRACK** AND HIS HAND-PICKED **STYGIANS...**

"...FELT AGAIN THE YOUNGER ARMS OF **N'YAGA THE SHAMAN,** BEARING ME AWAY AS MY FATHER **FELL IN BATTLE...!***

*ISSUE #59. --ROY.

47

"BUT, MOST *VIVIDLY* OF ALL, I BEHELD A SCENE THAT *NEVER* WAS:

"MY *TRIUMPHAL RETURN* TO ASGALUN-- AT *MY FATHER'S SIDE!*

"IT'S A SCENE I'VE DREAMT *BEFORE*, YET THOUGHT COULD NEVER BE *TRUE*...

...TILL *NIM-KARRAK* SWORE TO ME MY FATHER *DIDN'T* DIE YEARS AGO, BUT WAS TAKEN *ALIVE* BACK TO *STYGIA'S* CAPITAL!

BUT IT *WAS* YEARS AGO, REMEMBER.

PERHAPS CONAN WOULD SAY *MORE*: HOW NIM-KARRAK MIGHT HAVE *LIED* TO SAVE HIS HIDE, EVEN THOUGH BÊLIT WISHES TO THINK HE DID *NOT*.

BUT, JUST THEN--

GODDESS--!

SHIP HO!

THEN, BE- CAUSE THE TIGRESS *IS* A *PIRATE* SHIP, AFTER ALL...

...CONAN AND BÊLIT HAVE NO MORE TIME TO *MUSE*.

FALL TO, YOU LUBBERS!

THERE'S *BOOTY* TO BE HAD THIS FINE NIGHT!

AND, FROM EVERY *NOOK AND CRANNY* OF THE SHIP, AS IF HER VERY *BOARDS* HAD SPRUNG TO LIFE--

--THE *BLACK CORSAIRS* POUR FORTH, BRANDISH- ING *WAR-CRIES* AS READILY AS *SPEARS* AND *SHIELDS!*

SHE'S *STYGIAN*, ALL RIGHT, BÊLIT! AND NOW THAT SHE'S *SEEN* US, SHE'S TRYING TO *RUN* FOR IT.

NO STYGIAN SHIP EVER *MADE* CAN OUTSTRIP MY *TIGRESS*!

THE GODS ARE *WITH* US! ORDINARILY, I'D LOVE TO SEND HER TO THE *BOTTOM*...

BUT TONIGHT, I'LL *SPARE* ANY MAN WHO CAN TELL US ABOUT KING CTESPHON'S COURT AT *LUXUR*!

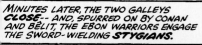

MINUTES LATER, THE TWO GALLEYS CLOSE -- AND, SPURRED ON BY CONAN AND BÊLIT, THE EBON WARRIORS ENGAGE THE SWORD-WIELDING *STYGIANS*.

THEY NEITHER KNOW NOR CARE *WHY* A STYGIAN SHIP IS SO *FAR* FROM ITS SHORE-HUGGING WAYS...

...BUT MERELY *HEW* AND *CUT*, AS IF MEN WERE *STALKS OF GRAIN*!

AND, MOST *FEARSOME* OF ALL IS *BÊLIT* -- WHO SEES IN EACH DYING STYGIAN FACE THE VISAGE OF ONE WHO MAY HAVE *HARMED HER FATHER*!

AT LAST, ONLY THE MOST NOBLE-LOOKING OF THE DEFENDERS STILL STANDS...

THROW DOWN YOUR *SWORD*, SET-WORSHIPPER, AND WE'LL *SPARE* YOU, IN EXCHANGE FOR KNOWLEDGE OF *LUXUR*!

BEFORE SUCH AS *YOU* GETS AUGHT FROM *ME* --

-- I'LL WRITHE BEFORE THE COILED PEDESTAL OF *SET* -- IN THE SERPENT-PIT-- OF *HELLLLLL*☀

CROM!

WHAT'S *WRONG*, MY BARBARIAN?

THESE *STYGIANS*! THEY MAKE MY *SKIN* CRAWL, WITH THEIR WORSHIP OF A *SNAKE-GOD*.

AND THE WAY THIS ONE *SLEW HIMSELF* PUSHING HIMSELF ON MY *BLADE*!

I MIGHT *FALL IN BATTLE* RATHER THAN SURRENDER-- BUT DAMNED IF I'D TAKE MY *OWN LIFE*!

YOUR WAYS ARE NOT LIKE *THEIRS*, OUTLANDER.

WHO IN THE NAME OF DARK *DERKETA*--?

I DON'T KNOW JUST *WHO* IT IS, *BÊLIT*...

...BUT, I'LL *WAGER* YOU DON'T END UP *LIKING* HER!

PLEASE-- DO NOT *KILL* ME, CORSAIRS!

I AM *NO* STYGIAN!

I AM ONLY...*NEFTHA*...!

WHOEVER YOU ARE, WHAT'S A *PALE-SKINNED* GIRL DOING ON A *STYGIAN RIG*?

DON'T YOU *KNOW*? CAN'T YOU *GUESS*?

THOUGH I HAVE A STYGIAN NAME, I WAS BORN OF *ZINGARAN* PARENTS, WHO *ENDED THEIR LIVES* IN LUXUR...

...AS *SLAVES*!

THIS MAN-- *BEKHET*, A NOBLE OF THE KING'S COURT-- WAS GOING INTO *EXILE*, AND TAKING ME AND MUCH ROYAL LOOT *WITH* HIM.

EXILE? *WHY*?

FOR PLOTTING TO *KILL KING CTESPHON*, WHOM MANY STYGIAN NOBLES THINK A *WEAKLING*!

AND ARE THEY *RIGHT*?

YES. HE SITS *GUARDED* DAY AND NIGHT IN HIS GREAT PALACE AT THE FAR END OF THE *RIVER STYX*.

NOT EVEN THE THREAT OF AN *HYBORIAN INVASION* COULD GET HIM TO STIR FORTH TO--*AHH*!

HERE IS WHAT I SOUGHT ON BEKHET'S BODY...

A *SET-CHARM*!

THOUGH I *LOATHE* THE STYGIANS' SNAKE-WORSHIP, I'VE ALWAYS *FANCIED* THIS.

AND, SINCE THERE'S SO MUCH *OTHER* TREASURE ABOARD, I HOPE YOU'LL LET ME *KEEP* IT...

...SINCE MITRA *KNOWS*, THE STYGIAN DOGS HAVE LEFT ME *LITTLE ELSE*...

...NOT EVEN *DIGNITY*.

I THINK WE CAN *SPARE* YOUR LITTLE TRINKET, GIRL.

OH, *THANK* YOU, MILORD! I--I CAN BE OF *COMFORT* TO YOU ON WHATEVER *VOYAGE* YOU MAKE...!

NOW *HOLD IT* RIGHT THERE!

CONAN'S *MY* MAN-- AND *I'M* CAPTAIN OF THIS SHIP, NOT *HE!*

THE GIRL MEANT *NO HARM,* BÊLIT. SHE DIDN'T *KNOW.*

WELL, SHE'D BEST *LEARN* QUICKLY!

PLEASE... I DO NOT *MEAN* TO OFFEND.

I HAVE SERVED THE PERVERSE WHIMS OF *BEKHET* SO LONG... I HARDLY KNOW WHAT TO *SAY* TO KINDER SOULS.

BUT, I HEARD YOU SPEAK OF *LUXUR* BEFORE... STYGIA'S *CAPITAL...*

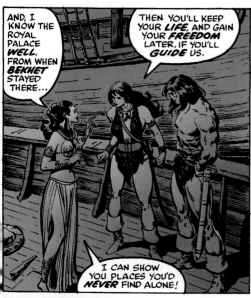

AND, I KNOW THE ROYAL PALACE *WELL,* FROM WHEN *BEKHET* STAYED THERE...

THEN YOU'LL KEEP YOUR *LIFE,* AND GAIN YOUR *FREEDOM* LATER, IF YOU'LL *GUIDE* US.

I CAN SHOW YOU PLACES YOU'D *NEVER* FIND ALONE!

SOON AFTERWARD, THE STYGIAN GALLEY *BURNS* LIKE A SHORT-LIVED *BEACON,* THEN SINKS INTO THE ROLLING, NIGHTED *SEA...*

AND *CONAN?*

HE RECALLS HIS ALL-BUT-FORGOTTEN *NIGHTMARE,* AND WONDERS *HOW LONG* BEFORE THOTH-AMON'S DREAM-PROPHECY FOR THE *TIGRESS* COMES TRUE.

A *DAY*... A *LIFETIME*... OR *NEVER.*

AS FOR *NEFTHA,* SHE HAS SALVAGED ONE THING *BESIDES* A GOLDEN CHARM FROM THE DOOMED VESSEL:

A *LYRE,* ON WHICH SHE PLAYS AND SINGS LIKE AN *ANGEL...*

BUT, SINCE SHE KNOWS NO TONGUE SAVE *STYGIAN*, IT IS ONLY THE *VOICE* AND THE *MELODIES* THAT THE CIMMERIAN CAN APPRECIATE.

AT LEAST, SO *BÊLIT* HOPES, AS SHE SILENTLY GLOWERS.

THEN, ON A GLORIOUS *FULL-MOON NIGHT*, WHEN ORDINARILY A PIRATE SHIP WOULD STAY *FAR AND CLEAR* OF ANY FORTIFIED SHORE...

...THE *TIGRESS* BOLDLY SAILS TO WITHIN ONLY A *CATAPULT'S HURLING* OF *KHEMI*, STYGIA'S MAJOR *PORT*...

...AND, LIKE SILENT *DRAGONFLIES* SKIMMING THE SURFACE, A *TRIO OF LONGBOATS* MAKE FOR THE *ROW OF VESSELS* IN FRONT OF THE SEEMINGLY SLUMBERING CITY.

WELL, THERE THEY *ARE*, GIRL-- THE *BLACK WALLS OF KHEMI*--

--THOUGH I'VE NEVER KNOWN IF, BY THAT NAME, THE STYGIANS MEAN THE *REAL* WALLS -- OR THEIR DARK *WARSHIPS*, THUS ARRAYED!

THEY MEAN... *BOTH*.

YET, REMEMBER WHAT I'VE *TOLD* YOU: THIS NIGHT, OF ALL NIGHTS, IS THE EVE OF A *HOLY FESTIVAL* DEVOTED TO THAT DEVIL-SERPENT *SET*.

I SUPPOSE CIVILIZED RACES ARE *ALL* MAD, IN THEIR WAY.

NO ONE *STIRS FORTH* ON THIS NIGHT-- NOT EVEN TO *GUARD* THEIR NAVY!

I JUST HOPE YOU'RE *RIGHT*, GIRL...

"FOR, OTHERWISE, *THREE LONG-BOATS*--COM-MANDED BY BÊLIT, M'GORA, COULD NEVER HOPE TO ACCOMPLISH WHAT *WE* HAVE IN MIND.

"STILL, *KHEMI* BLOCKS OUR PASSAGE TO *LUXUR*. SO WE'VE NO *CHOICE!*"

THUS, WITH MUFFLED OARS, THE THREE LONGBOATS GLIDE NIGH-SILENTLY TOWARD THE NEAREST OF THE DARK SHIPS.

AND, IN HER OWN WAY, THE GIRL CALLED NEFTHA WAS *RIGHT:*

THERE ARE *NO* GUARDS ON BOARD THE STYGIAN WARSHIPS...

YET, THEY ARE *STILL* FAR FROM *UNATTENDED...!*

HRONK!

MANNANAN AND LIR!

CONAN'S STARTLED OUTBURST IS ODDLY *FITTING...*

FOR, MANNANAN AND LIR, *CIMMERIAN GODS* HANDED DOWN FROM *ATLANTEAN FOREBEARS,* WERE *SEA-GODS* ONCE...

AND SURELY IT IS EITHER *GOD* OR *DEMON* WHOSE LONG SNOUT AND RAZOR-SHARP FANGS NOW *SWEEP* ACROSS THE BOBBING LONGBOAT--!

NO! DAGON HELP ME!

WHAT THE *DEVIL*--?

I'VE *HEARD* OF SUCH DRAGONS-- CALLED FORTH BY *STYGIAN WIZARDS*--

BUT, I NEVER *DREAMED*--!

DREAMS! I'M *DONE* WITH DREAMS--

--AND WITH TOOTHSOME *NIGHTMARES!*

MY *SWORD* WON'T STOP THAT THING--

BUT, CROM TAKE ME, IT WILL *KNOW* IT SLEW A *MAN* TONIGHT!

BUT THEN, AS *CAVERNOUS JAWS* GAPE WIDELY, AND *FETID BREATH* ALL BUT OVERWHELMS...

WHAT--? IT *STOPPED*-- STOPPED *COLD!*

AND *NOW*-- IT'S MAKING FOR *ANOTHER* BOAT!

GRONK!

M'GORA! *WATCH OUT!!*

BUT, *HOW* DOES ONE WATCH OUT FOR--

--SEVENTY TONS OF QUASI-REPTILLIAN *FURY?*

READY, CORSAIRS?

BY ISHTAR, THAT OUT-SIZED LIZARD *WON'T* KILL M'GORA AND THE OTHERS IF *WE* CAN PREVENT IT!

WE ARE *READY,* GODDESS.

HROWRR

AND HERE IT COMES!

CONAN! WHAT ARE YOU--?

BÊLIT IS MY *WOMAN.*

HE SAYS *NO MORE,* AS IF NO MORE *NEEDS* SAYING...

...BUT HURLS HIMSELF *INTO* AND *UNDER* THE COLD WATERS, AS HEEDLESS OF *DANGER* AS THOUGH HE THINKS HE IS *IMMORTAL.*

HE DOES *NOT.*

BUT, A MOMENT LATER, WHEN THE MONSTER HURLS ITSELF *UP* AND TOWARD BÊLIT'S *LONG-BOAT*--

--AN *UNWANTED RIDER* IS CLAMBERING WILDLY UP ITS SCALE-RIDGED *BACK*--

--AND, EVEN AS IT FINALLY *SENSES* THE ADDED *WEIGHT*--

--EVEN AS IT STRAINS TO *TWIST* ITS LONG NECK SO IT CAN *SEE* ITS ATTACKER--

HALF ITS SIGHT GOES SUDDENLY *BLACK!*

THEN, MADDENED WITH *PAIN* AND *RAGE*, THE CREATURE *DIVES*--

--AS IF THERE IS *SOLACE* FOR ITS AGONY ONLY IN *NIGHTED DEPTHS* WHENCE SOME *UN-KNOWN SORCERER'S SPELL* HAS CALLED IT!

55

FOR LONG MOMENTS, THE WATERS *CHURN* WHERE MAN AND MONSTER HAVE VANISHED; THEN, AT LENGTH, THEY BEGIN TO *SUBSIDE.*

TORN WITH *ANGUISH,* BÊLIT IS ABOUT TO *THROW ASIDE* HER GLEAMING CUTLASS AND *DIVE AFTER* AFTER THEM INTO THE BECKONING BLACKNESS, WHEN *SUDDENLY--*

GODDESS-- BEHOLD--

IT IS-- *AMRA!*

ISHTAR BE PRAISED!

ARE YOU *ALL RIGHT,* MY LOVER?

I-- *THINK* SO-- THOUGH MY *LUNGS* ACHE NEAR TO *BURSTING!*

THE *DRAGON--?*

IT'S *RISEN,* TOO-- BUT HEADED OUT BLINDLY TO *SEA!*

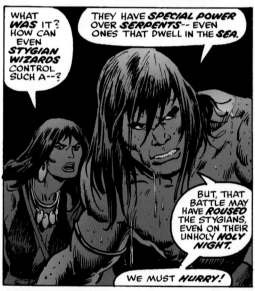

WHAT *WAS* IT? HOW CAN EVEN *STYGIAN WIZARDS* CONTROL SUCH A--?

THEY HAVE *SPECIAL POWER* OVER *SERPENTS*-- EVEN ONES THAT DWELL IN THE *SEA.*

BUT, THAT BATTLE MAY HAVE *ROUSED* THE STYGIANS, EVEN ON THEIR UNHOLY *HOLY NIGHT.*

WE MUST *HURRY!*

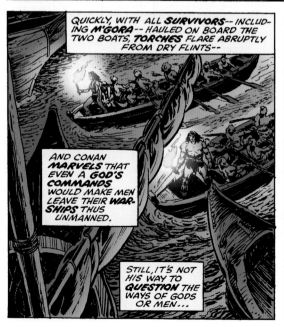

QUICKLY, WITH ALL *SURVIVORS*-- INCLUDING M'GORA-- HAULED ON BOARD THE TWO BOATS, *TORCHES* FLARE ABRUPTLY FROM DRY FLINTS--

AND CONAN *MARVELS* THAT EVEN A *GOD'S COMMANDS* WOULD MAKE MEN LEAVE THEIR *WARSHIPS* THUS UNMANNED.

STILL, IT'S NOT HIS WAY TO *QUESTION* THE WAYS OF GODS OR MEN...

AND SO, WITHIN MINUTES, A *WOODEN* ROW OF BLACK WALLS BURN LURIDLY, REDLY, BEFORE THOSE *OTHER* BLACK WALLS OF *STONE...*

56

NOW, AT LAST, THE STYGIANS ARE ROUSED TO ACTION--

--AS THEY POUR FORTH YELLING INTO THE SCARLET NIGHT!

DESPERATELY, THEY STRIVE TO PUT OUT THE RAGING FIRES-- AND, IN TIME, THEY WILL SALVAGE ALL BUT A FEW OF THEIR SHIPS...

BY THAT TIME, TWO STREAKING LONGBOATS WILL LONG SINCE HAVE REACHED THE TIGRESS...

...WHICH WILL BE OFF TOWARD THE OPEN SEA UNDER M'GORA'S COMMAND TO RENDEZVOUS WITH THEIR CAPTAIN AT A DIFFERENT TIME AND PLACE.

AND CONAN?

TWO DECADES HENCE, HE WILL REMEMBER WITH FONDNESS HOW HE MADE THE STYGIANS HOWL, WHEN HE CREPT WITH HIS BLACK CORSAIRS TO THE VERY BASTIONS OF THE SEA-WASHED CASTLE OF KHEMI, AND BURNED THE GALLEONS LYING AT ANCHOR THERE.

BUT TONIGHT, HE STANDS IN THE SHADOWS ALONGSIDE BÊLIT AND THE SLAVE-GIRL NEFTHA...

...AND THINKS GRIMLY HOW LONG AND DANGER-LADEN IS THE TORTUOUS ROAD TO SERPENT-RIDDLED LUXUR!

NEXT ISSUE: THE HAWK-RIDERS OF HARAKHT!

"Know, O prince, that between the years when the oceans drank Atlantis and the gleaming cities, and the rise of the sons of Aryas, there was an Age undreamed of, when shining kingdoms lay spread across the world like blue mantles beneath the stars.
"Hither came Conan, the Cimmerian, black-haired, sullen-eyed, sword in hand, a thief, a reaver, a slayer, with gigantic melancholies and gigantic mirth, to tread the jeweled thrones of the Earth under his sandaled feet."
—The Nemedian Chronicles.

STAN LEE PRESENTS: CONAN THE BARBARIAN™

THE HAWK-RIDERS OF HARAKHT!

THEY ARE BURNING, THOSE WARSHIPS MEN CALL THE "BLACK WALLS OF KHEMI"!..

AND, THOUGH HE SAYS NOTHING, CONAN THE CIMMERIAN FEELS A SURGE OF JOY THRILL HIS HEART, BELOW HIS GRIMLY SILENT EXTERIOR... FOR HE KNOWS THAT, OF SUCH HOLOCAUSTS, LEGENDS ARE BORN.

AS FOR BÊLIT, WHOSE FATHER WAS DETHRONED IN PROUD ASGALUN BY THESE SAME STYGIANS, YEARS AGO-- SHE FEELS NOTHING BUT A FIERCE HATRED FOR THEM WHICH DOES NOT ALLOW OF A SMILE.

ONLY THE SLAVE GIRL NEFTHA HAS FEELINGS WHICH CANNOT BE READ...

AND, WHAT MATTER THE THOUGHTS OF A ZINGARA-BORN THRALL, COMPARED TO THOSE OF THE QUEEN OF THE BLACK COAST AND HER BLACK-MANED LION...?

ROY THOMAS
WRITER/EDITOR

JOHN BUSCEMA & ERNIE CHAN
ILLUSTRATORS

JOHN COSTANZA
letterer

Featuring CHARACTERS CREATED BY ROBERT E. HOWARD

AT LAST, *SHEMITISH ACCENTS* BREAK THE FLAME-SPECKED TABLEAU...

REVENGE IS *SWEET,* EVEN WHEN FAR FROM *COMPLETE.*

AYE, WOMAN... BUT, WE'D BEST BE *GOING...*

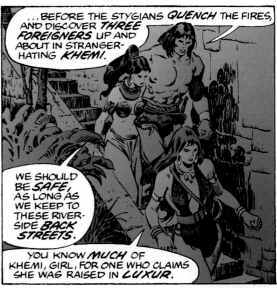

...BEFORE THE STYGIANS *QUENCH* THE FIRES, AND DISCOVER *THREE FOREIGNERS* UP AND ABOUT IN STRANGER-HATING *KHEMI.*

WE SHOULD BE *SAFE,* AS LONG AS WE KEEP TO THESE RIVER-SIDE *BACK STREETS.*

YOU KNOW *MUCH* OF KHEMI, GIRL, FOR ONE WHO CLAIMS SHE WAS RAISED IN *LUXUR.*

AS I'VE *TOLD* YOU: MY DEAD MASTER *BEKHET* BROUGHT ME HERE OFTEN, ON MISSIONS FOR *KING CTESPHON.*

YOU'VE NO *TREACHERY* TO FEAR FROM ME -- FOR, AM I NOT ALWAYS WITHIN *SWORD'S REACH?*

AND YOU'LL *STAY* THAT WAY, TILL WE REACH *LUXUR.*

BUT NOW-- *YONDER* MUST BE THE *MERCHANT'S SHOP* WHICH YOU TOLD US ABOUT!

I'M SURPRISED *YOU* DON'T KNOW ANY TRADERS HERE, *BÊLIT.*

YOU KNOW THE STYGIANS *DISCOURAGE* TRADING... AND THUS, *PIRACY.*

FOR AN OUTLANDER MERELY TO *WALK THE STREETS* AFTER DARK IS TO INVITE *DEATH.*

SO, *I* DEAL WITH THE GREEDIER, MORE PRACTICAL MEN OF *ARGOS* AND POINTS NORTH.

AH! A *CANDLE'S* BEING LIT WITHIN!

IT WOULD *NOT* HAVE, IF YOU'D NOT USED THE *SECRET KNOCK* OF WHICH MY FORMER *MASTER* ONCE SPOKE.

EH? SET'S NAME-- WHO *IS* IT THAT KNOCKS ON THIS *HOLY NIGHT?*

WE'VE THINGS TO *TRADE.*

PLAGUE TAKE YOU! *NAME* WHAT YOU'D TRADE, AND IT HAD BEST BE *WORTHWHILE,* TO HAUL ME OUT OF *BED!*

HOW ABOUT *THIS*, SHARP-TONGUE:

YOUR *LIFE*, FOR AN *OPENED DOOR!*

:ULP!: THAT, ER, *SEEMS* FAIR, MISTRESS...!

NOW, WE'LL TELL YOU WHAT WE'VE COME TO--

I CAN *SEE:* THAT ONE WEARS THE *SLAVE-NECKLACE* OF ONE WHO WAS A PLAYTHING OF THE *NOBILITY.*

THEY'D FEED ME TO THE *STREET-SERPENTS* IF I BOUGHT *HER.*

WE'RE *NOT* HERE TO SELL *WOMEN*, FLESHMONGER.

JUST *LISTEN*-- AND SPEAK WHEN *SPOKEN* TO!

OH, *YES*-- SURELY A MOST *ADMIRABLE* COURSE, MASTER!

THAT'S *BETTER!* WE SEE YOUR *BOAT* OUTSIDE -- ALL LOADED WITH GOODS FOR A TRIP UPRIVER TO *LUXUR*, NO DOUBT.

UH, *YES.* IT--

THEN, *PREPARE* THINGS--FOR, YOU'LL HAVE *THREE* PASSENGERS BESIDES THE GOODS YOU BRING THE *ROYAL COURT.*

BUT, *I* WASN'T PERSONALLY GOING TO--

YOU ARE *NOW!*

IT ISN'T *FAIR!* WHY MUST YOU PICK ON *ME?*

I'M ONLY A POOR *TRADESMAN*, TRYING TO EARN AN HONEST LIVING FROM *SPICES* AND *SLAVES!*

MY HEART *BLEEDS* FOR YOU.

NOW, ABOUT OUR *DISGUISES...!*

AT **DAWN'S** FIRST SIGN, A LONG **BARGE** BEGINS ITS SLOW, SERPENTINE PATH *UPRIVER.*

THE **RIVER STYX** IS QUIET, PEACEFUL... AND THOSE HYBORIANS WHO ALREADY REFER TO IT AS THE "*RIVER OF DEATH*" WOULD SCARCELY FEEL THE SAME, WERE THEY TO SEE IT *FIRSTHAND.*

THOUGH IT'S SAID **KING CTESPHON** LOCKS HIMSELF AWAY IN DARK TOWERS FOR FEAR OF **ASSASSINS'** KNIVES, STILL HE MUST HAVE HIS **PLEASURES.**

THERE MUST BE **KUSHITE IVORY** AND **ARGOSSEAN MARBLE** FOR HIS PALACE... **SLAVES** OF EVERY CLIME AND COLOR, FOR BOTH HIS HOUSE-HOLD AND HIS **HAREM.**

NO DOUBT, THE DOZEN INDEN-TURED **ROWERS** OF THE BARGE ASSUME THAT THE PAIR OF **DUSKY WOMEN** ON BOARD ARE IN THE LATTER CATEGORY...

...AND THEY'RE TOO BUSY ROWING TO SEE THAT HASTY **SKIN-PAINTING** HAS BEEN DONE ON THEM, IF NOT ON THEIR **KEEPER.**

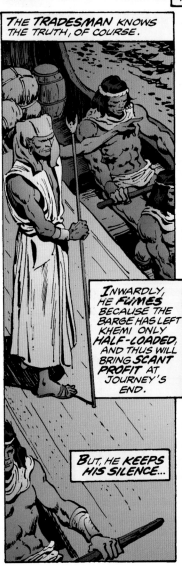

THE **TRADESMAN** KNOWS THE TRUTH, OF COURSE.

INWARDLY, HE **FUMES**, BECAUSE THE BARGE HAS LEFT KHEMI ONLY **HALF-LOADED,** AND THUS WILL BRING **SCANT PROFIT** AT JOURNEY'S END.

BUT, HE **KEEPS HIS SILENCE...**

...SINCE HE'S NO DESIRE TO BECOME A **MEAL** FOR THE SACRED, SCALY **SONS OF SET** WHO KEEP AN IMPLACABLE EYE ON THE BARGE'S PROGRESS...

HE WONDERS: ARE SUCH AS THESE **TRULY** THE REPRE-SENTATIVES OF THE GOD **SET** ON EARTH, AS ARE THE GREAT **SNAKES** WHICH FREELY ROAM THE STREETS OF KHEMI?

AND, IF SO, WHAT OF THE HERON-LIKE *IBIS BIRDS* WHICH TREK THE MARSHES, JUST BEYOND *REACH* OF THE REPTILIANS?

THE TRADESMAN SEEMS TO RECALL THAT *IBIS*, TOO, WAS THE NAME OF A *STYGIAN GOD* ONCE.

BUT, THAT WAS *LONG AGO*, IF TRUE.

ONCE, THE GIRL *NEFTHA* BREAKS HER SILENCE TO SPEAK OF IBIS-- YET IT IS AS IF HE WERE BUT A *FAIRY-TALE* GOD, WHOSE PRIESTS WERE *CAST DOWN* BEFORE HER BIRTH.

BÊLIT, RECALLING A RECENT ENCOUNTER WITH *KARANTHES*, PRIEST OF IBIS, COULD VOUCH THAT HIS SERVANTS STILL HAVE *SOME* WIZARDLY POWER...

BUT SHE DOES *NOT*.

IT IS LEFT TO *CONAN* TO SILENTLY RECALL THAT KARANTHES HAD ASKED HIM AND BÊLIT AND RED SONJA TO GO SOUTH TO STYGIA ON A *MISSION* FOR HIM AND HIS LONG-BEAKED GOD.

THEY ALL *REFUSED*... YET HERE NOW *TWO* OF THEM ARE.

COINCIDENCE? PROBABLY.

AND SO THE JOURNEY *CONTINUES ON*, THE SCENERY CHANGING FROM MARSH TO PLAIN AND BACK AGAIN...

BUT EVER, THE MEASURED PACE OF THE ROWERS IS *SLOW* AND *STEADY*...

...TILL SUDDENLY, NEARLY *MIDWAY* 'TWIXT KHEMI AND LUXUR...

ALL RIGHT, YOU LOWLIFE SCUM! PAY YOUR DEBT TO *ME* AS YOU NEVER PAID THEM TO YOUR *CREDITORS*!

DOUBLE YOUR STROKE--IF YOU *VALUE YOUR HIDES*!

TRADESMAN! WHY THE *PANIC*?

I DON'T SEE *WHY*--

SHHH! THAT IS BECAUSE YOU DON'T KNOW *STYGIA*, OUTLANDER...

LOOK OVER YONDER...!

EH? WHAT THE DEVIL ARE YOU *TALKING* ABOUT, MAN?

I SUPPOSE THAT *FEW* OUTSIDE STYGIA HAVE HEARD MUCH ABOUT *HARAKHT*, CITY OF THE *HAWK-GOD.*

NOMINALLY, IT IS SUBJECT TO THE *CROWN--* BUT IN REALITY, IT GOES *ITS OWN WAY:*

WHY DOES KING CTESPHON *ALLOW* IT TO?

BECAUSE IT LIES HALFWAY BETWEEN *KHEMI* AND *LUXUR.*

IF IT *FELL,* THE WAY WOULD BE OPEN FOR A *SHEMITE ARMY* TO SPLIT THIS LAND IN *HALF* IN TIME OF *WAR!*

BETTER A STRONG *STYGIAN* VASSAL--THAN *FOREIGN HORDES.*

SOUND ENOUGH! BUT, WHY DO YOU *MUTE* YOUR MEN IN ROWING PAST--?

CROM! WHAT--?

SHADES OF SET!

A LONG GREY *SHADOW* TURNS THE CIMMERIAN'S EYES *SKYWARD...*

...AND THEN HE NEED ASK *NO MORE QUESTIONS!*

NOR *COULD* HE, IF HE SO *DESIRED--*

FOR, THE SHRIEKING *TRADESMAN* IS THE FIRST TO *TOPPLE* BENEATH THE MARAUDERS' ARROWS--

--AND THE *RIVER STYX* YIELDS UP *NO SECRETS!*

BEFORE THE GIGANTIC *BIRDS OF PREY* AND THEIR FIERCE-EYED *HUMAN RIDERS*, THE SNOW-WHITE *IBIS* BIRDS TAKE NOISOME *WING*...

BUT, THE GREAT *STYGIAN CROCODILES* MERELY MAKE FOR THE *WATER*, AS IF THE ATTACKERS' ARROWS SING A SONG THEY'VE HEARD *BEFORE*.

ABOVE THE SHRILL CRIES OF THE GREAT HAWKS, THE *SHOUTED COMMANDS* OF MEN CAN SCARCELY BE *HEARD*...

BEACH HER, JACKALS OF KHEMI-- *OR DIE!*

SKREEE!

STILL, THE *FINAL* WORD RINGS LOUD AND CLEAR--

--LOUD ENOUGH FOR STARK, UNREASONING *TERROR* TO GRASP THE ROWERS BY THE THROAT--

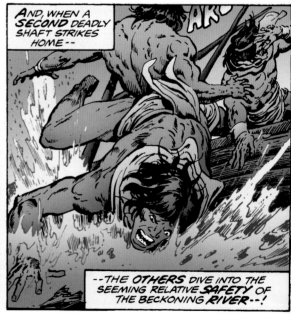

AND, WHEN A *SECOND* DEADLY SHAFT STRIKES HOME--

--THE *OTHERS* DIVE INTO THE SEEMING RELATIVE *SAFETY* OF THE BECKONING *RIVER*--!

THE RIVER-DRAGONS ARE THERE... WAITING.

BY THIS TIME, THE TWO CORSAIRS HAVE ALREADY RECOVERED FROM THEIR INITIAL SHOCK...

BÊLIT! TIME TO SHED THESE CIVILIZED TRAPPINGS!

AYE, MY LOVER! WOULD THAT I COULD SHED THESE DUSKY DYES AS EASILY!

BUT, WHAT WE REALLY NEED RIGHT NOW-- IS SHIELDS!

THERE ARE BRONZED ONES FROM SHEM THERE IN THE STERN! I TOOK NOTE OF WHERE THE TRADESMAN STORED THEM!

DO YOU THINK I DID LESS??

HERE!

THANKS! NOW, IF ONE OF THOSE WINGED DEVILS WILL JUST SWOOP LOW ENOUGH--!

CONAN! WHAT ABOUT ME??

DAMN YOUR HIDE, GIRL-- I CAN'T MOVE FREELY WITH YOU HUGGING MY MIDDLE!

GET BACK UNDER THE CANOPY, WHERE NO ARROW'S LIKE TO FIND YOU!

I'LL TELL YOU WHEN TO COME OUT, IF--

HE STARTS TO SAY: "IF I'M STILL ALIVE!"

JUST THEN, THE LAST OARSMAN STILL ON BOARD FINALLY GIVES WAY TO HIS FEARS--

--AND RUSHES FORTH FROM HIS HIDING PLACE--

--ONLY TO FEEL THE SHARP-CLAWED FURY OF A HUGE PREDATOR!

YYYAAA!

MEANWHILE, HOWEVER, A SECOND OF THE FIVE MARAUDERS MEETS A FAR DIFFERENT KIND OF FOE...

BY ISHTAR, I'VE FOUGHT MAN-WORMS AND DEMONS FROM THE DARK IN MY DAY--

SKRE--

--AND I'LL NOT FLEE FROM SOME FALCON THAT'S FEASTED ON TWO MANY QUAIL!

THE SWEEPING SCIMITAR WOUNDS THE GREAT HAWK, WHICH FALLS BACK IN ITS UNACCUSTOMED PAIN--

YET, ITS SHRIEK MERELY SERVES TO MASK THE BEAT OF VAST WINGS BEHIND THE SHEMITE SHE-PIRATE...

...TILL STRONG TALONS GRASP HER SWORD-ARM IN AN UNBREAKABLE GRIP--

--AND BEAR HER SUDDENLY SKYWARD!

YOU STINKING STYGIAN SCUM!

BÊLIT!!

CONAN-- MASTER-- WAIT!

DON'T LEAVE ME! THEY'LL KILL YOU, TOO!

BUT, THE BARBARIAN IS DEAF TO ALL PLEAS--

--AS, CASTING HIS SHIELD, AS WELL AS CAUTION, TO THE WIND--

--HIS WARRIOR'S MIND INSTANTLY PLOTS THE TRAJECTORY OF A SWOOPING HAWK-RIDER--

-- WHO COULD NOT CHANGE HIS COURSE IN TIME, IF HE WISHED TO!

ALL RIGHT, YOU COWARDLY DOG--

YOU *WANTED* A FIGHT--!

--WITH PANTHERISH SPEED, HE *DUCKS UNDER* THOSE RAKING TALONS--

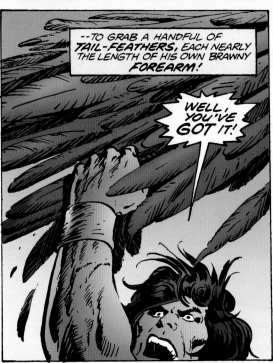

--TO GRAB A HANDFUL OF *TAIL-FEATHERS,* EACH NEARLY THE LENGTH OF HIS OWN BRAWNY *FOREARM!*

WELL, YOU'VE *GOT* IT!

THE ONLY THING HE *CANNOT* RETAIN AS HE CLAWS HIS WAY ATOP THE STREAKING BIRD--IS HIS *SWORD!*

PIVOTING, THE HAWK-RIDER *SMILES* GRIMLY, TO SEE IT *FALL.*

THEN, AS THE GREAT HAWK *RISES* AGAIN, LEAVING THE STYX *FAR BELOW*--

--HE SWEEPS A WIDE, DEATHLY *ARC,* WHICH CONAN CANNOT ENTER WITH NEITHER SWORD OR SHIELD OF HIS *OWN.*

FIERCELY, HE CLINGS TO THE MONSTER'S BACK-- AND WAITS HIS *CHANCE.*

IT IS **NOT** LONG IN COMING.

ONE MOMENT, THE STYGIAN'S SWORD-ARM IS **STILL**--ENDING **ONE** LETHAL ARC AND POISED TO BEGIN **ANOTHER**...

THE **NEXT,** AND HIS WRIST IS **GRASPED** BY CONAN'S GREAT HAND--AND THE HAWK-RIDER CAN **SENSE** HIS SHEER **POWER,** RADIATING OUTWARD AS THOUGH IT WERE THE HAND OF THE **SUN-GOD** HIMSELF!

IT TAKES ONLY A **SECOND** STRONG HAND, CLUTCHING HIS **THROAT,** FOR THE STYGIAN TO KNOW THAT HE IS A **DOOMED MAN**...!

THEN, WITH ALMOST THE SPEED OF **LIGHTNING**--

--CONAN IS THE **ONLY** RIDER ON THE BACK OF THE **ENORMOUS** HAWK.

EVEN AS THE STYGIAN HURTLES DOWNWARD, CONAN SPIES THE DEAD TRADESMAN'S **BARGE** FAR BELOW, SURROUNDED BY FEEDING, SPLASHING **CROCODILES.**

HE KNOWS **BÊLIT** IS NOT AMONG THEIR VICTIMS--THOUGH HE CANNOT BE SO SURE ABOUT THE SLAVE GIRL CALLED **NEFTHA**

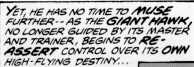

YET, HE HAS NO TIME TO *MUSE* FURTHER-- AS THE *GIANT HAWK,* NO LONGER GUIDED BY ITS MASTER AND TRAINER, BEGINS TO *RE-ASSERT* CONTROL OVER ITS *OWN* HIGH-FLYING DESTINY...

CROM!

FOR ONE BRIEF INSTANT, THE CIMMERIAN IS NEARLY *TOSSED OFF* THE BIRD'S BROAD BACK--

THEN, FEELING AN *UNSURE* HAND AT ITS REINS -- AN *UNFAMILIAR* WEIGHT ON ITS BACK -- IT STARTS A MADDENING, WIND-LASHING *DIVE*--

DAMN YOU, BIRD!

--AND CONAN LEARNS THAT EVEN THE *BRAVEST* OF WARRIORS CAN BE BETRAYED BY HIS OWN *STOMACH!*

NO USE, NOW, TO TRY WITH INEFFECTUAL *REINS* TO CONTROL THE HUGE FALCON...

CONAN KNOWS THAT, SOONER OR LATER, THE BIRD *WILL* THROW HIM OFF -- AND THE *ODDS* ARE THAT IT WILL BE OVER *DRY LAND!*

BETTER TO SLAY IT NOW, HIS INSTINCTS TELL HIM, WHILE THERE IS STILL THE *RIVER STYX* DIRECTLY BELOW.

--IF THE STYX *IS* STILL BELOW!

CONAN HAS NO TIME TO *LOOK,* AS HIS TENSE SINEWS *STRAIN* AGAINST THE HAWK'S FIERCE MIGHT.

SHREEE

AND ALL THE WHILE IT STRIVES LIKE SOME *WILD, UNTAMED STALLION* TO HURL THE HATED *HUMAN* FROM ITS BACK -- AND GAIN ITS BLUE-BECKONING *FREEDOM.*

FOR CONAN, THE **MOMENT OF TRUTH** IS NEAR --FOR, EVEN **HIS** BRAWNY ARMS CANNOT FOR LONG **HOLD BACK** THIS CREATURE SO MUCH **LARGER** THAN HIMSELF--!

HE **MUST** SLAY IT NOW-- ERE HIS VERY **TENDONS** ARE STRAINED BEYOND ALL MORTAL ENDURANCE!

WITH A CRY MORE OF **AGONY** THAN OF RAGE OR TERROR, HE **TIGHTENS** HIS GRIP--

--AND SUDDENLY THE BIRD'S NECK GOES **SLACK!**

FOR A FLEETING MOMENT, THE HAWK **HOVERS** IN MID-AIR, AS IF IT COULD STAY THERE **FOREVER.**

THEN-- IT PLUMMETS **DOWNWARD** AT A SICKENING SPEED--

AND CONAN SEES TO HIS HORROR THAT THEY WERE **NO LONGER** DIRECTLY OVER THE **RIVER** ITSELF--

--BUT OVER THE REPTILE-INFESTED **MARSHLAND** ALONG ITS SIDE!

HAWK AND RIDER FALL *NEAR* TO EACH OTHER, AND THE BROKEN-NECKED BIRD IS *DEAD* ON *IMPACT*--

--AS SURELY ITS *CONQUEROR* WOULD BE, IF THE SWAMPY SHORELINE WERE AN *IOTA* *FIRMER*.

YET, WHEN THE FINAL SPLASHINGS AND THRASHINGS ARE DONE, THERE IS STILL *ONE* UNFAMILIAR SOUND THERE IN THE MARSH:

A MAN'S LABORED *BREATHING*.

THEN, A SOUND *NOT* NEW TO THE MARSHLAND: THE HALF-WALKING, HALF-SWIMMING GAIT OF A HUGE *CROCODILE*.

IT *STOPS*-- CAUTIOUS DIMLY OF A *SNARE*.

THE HUMAN THING BEFORE IT *DOES NOT MOVE*.

BUT, AS IT TAKES STILL *ANOTHER* STEP--

--THE RIVER'S *WINGED* DENIZENS TAKE FLIGHT-- AND NOT *SILENTLY*!

IT IS *THEIR* SHRILL CRIES THAT CAUSE CONAN'S *EYES* TO BLINK OPEN.

INSTANTLY, HE *RECALLS* ALL THAT HAS HAPPENED --AND RECOGNIZES THE *SOUND* OFF TO HIS *LEFT*--

--AS THE SLITHERING TREAD of *SCALY DEATH!*

COME AHEAD, YOU SON OF A--

CIVILIZED MEN, FACED WITH GAPING YARD-LONG JAWS AND TWIN ROWS OF GLEAMING FANGS, WOULD MOSTLY GROW *WEAK WITH FEAR...*

FEAR IS HARDLY *UNKNOWN* TO CONAN--AND YET, HE RESERVES HIS *GREATEST* FEAR FOR THOSE THINGS HE *CANNOT UNDERSTAND--* THINGS FROM *BEYOND.*

THIS GREAT *REPTILE,* THOUGH CAPABLE OF DEVOURING HIM ALMOST WHOLE, IS BUT AN *ANIMAL--*ANOTHER CREATURE NOT UNLIKE *HIMSELF* IN MANY WAYS--

--A BEAST WHICH USES *TEETH* AND *TALONS,* WHERE A *MAN* MUST USE--

--A GOOD SHARP *BLADE!*

HAH!

AND, IN THE END, IT IS THIS COMBINATION OF *COURAGE* AND *DESPERATION* WHICH PREVAILS, AS THE *METHODICAL* RISING AND FALLING OF CONAN'S KNIFE MINGLES WITH *THE* CROCODILE'S DEEP-THROATED SNORTING--

--AND THE FETID *WATERS* TURN CRIMSON WITH INHUMAN *BLOOD.*

EVEN AS THE MONSTER DIES, CONAN'S DANGER-HONED SENSES TELL HIM THAT NO *OTHER* RIVER-DRAGONS ARE CLOSE ENOUGH TO OVERTAKE HIM BEFORE HE CAN REACH *DRY, SOLID GROUND.*

YET, EVEN *THAT* SELF-PRESERVING THOUGHT IS ONLY IN THE *BACK* OF HIS MIND AT THIS MOMENT...

ALREADY, HIS THOUGHTS ARE OF *BÊLIT*-- HIS *MATE* -- STOLEN FROM HIM BY BEAK-MASKED *STYGIANS* RIDING GREAT, UNBELIEVABLE *HAWKS.*

IGNORING THE PAIN OF HIS VARIOUS WOUNDS, HE RISES TO HIS *FEET* --

--IN TIME TO SEE THE *FOUR SUR-VIVING HAWKS* IN THE DISTANCE, GRACEFULLY DESCENDING TOWARD THE MYSTERY-SHROUDED CITY CALLED *HARAKHT.*

THERE IS *NO QUESTION* WHETHER OR NOT CONAN WILL *FOLLOW* THEM THERE, TO TRY TO RETRIEVE THE *WOMAN HE LOVES.*

THE ONLY POSSIBLE QUESTIONS ARE, WHETHER HE WILL BE ABLE TO *FREE* HER, AND ESCAPE WITH HER AT HIS *SIDE* --

--OR ELSE, HOW MANY *STYGIANS* WILL DIE, SPRAWLED REDLY ACROSS HIS OWN HACKED AND LIFELESS BODY --!

NEXT ISSUE: **VENGEANCE IS MINE!**

"Know, O prince, that between the years when the oceans drank Atlantis and the gleaming cities, and the rise of the sons of Aryas, there was an Age undreamed of, when shining kingdoms lay spread across the world like blue mantles beneath the stars.
"Hither came Conan, the Cimmerian, black-haired, sullen-eyed, sword in hand, a thief, a reaver, a slayer, with gigantic melancholies and gigantic mirth, to tread the jeweled thrones of the Earth under his sandaled feet."
—The Nemedian Chronicles.

STAN LEE PRESENTS: CONAN THE BARBARIAN™

SWORDLESS IN STYGIA

ROY THOMAS ★ **JOHN BUSCEMA & ERNIE CHAN** ★ *J. COSTANZA* ★ **ARCHIE GOODWIN**
AUTHOR/EDITOR · ILLUSTRATORS · letterer · CONSULTING EDITOR

TO THE WEST: THE DYING SUN SPILLS ITS LAST LIFE'S-BLOOD OVER THE SEA-WASHED CASTLES OF *KHEMI*,

TO THE EAST: THE CITY CALLED *LUXUR* LIES EQUALLY FAR AWAY, AS IF UNAWARE THAT IT IS THE ULTIMATE DESTINATION OF A GREAT, BRONZED *CIMMERIAN*.

YET, IN THIS FROZEN INSTANT OF TIME, IT IS NEITHER TO *WEST* NOR TO *EAST* THAT CONAN TURNS HIS STEEL-BLUE EYES...

THEY GLARE *SOUTHWARD*-- AND SOUTHWARD *ONLY*--!

Featuring: WARRIORS, WOMEN, AND WIZARDS CREATED BY **ROBERT E. HOWARD**

AYE, SOUTHWARD-- WHERE THE DIM, FLUTTERING FIGURES OF *FOUR GIGANTIC FALCONS* ARE VANISHING--

--DESCENDING SLOWLY TOWARD THE WALLED ROOFS OF *HARAKHT,* CITY OF THE STYGIAN *HAWK-GOD.*

ONE OF THOSE GREAT BIRDS IS CARRYING THE SHE-PIRATE *BÊLIT* TO AN UNKNOWN FATE.

BUT, BÊLIT IS CONAN'S MATE-- HIS COMPANION ABOVE AND BELOW THE DECKS OF THE SEA-ROVING *TIGRESS* --

BEHIND HIM, HE HEARS THE *CROCODILES* FEASTING ON THE GRISLY REMAINS OF THEIR *SLAIN BROTHER...*

:...AS HIS SLOGGING *TREAD* DISTURBS SEVERAL *IBIS-BIRDS,* PREVIOUSLY HIDDEN BY DUSK AND REEDS.

SOMETHING ELSE IS THERE:

ONE OF THE *HEADDRESSES* WORN BY THOSE WHO RODE OF THE *BACKS* OF THE GREAT HAWKS!

THE MASK, NO DOUBT, OF THE ONE *CONAN SLEW!*

CONAN DOES NOT ASK IF *DESTINY* OR *BLIND LUCK* HAS BROUGHT HIM THIS UNEXPECTED BOUNTY.

HE MERELY *DONS* IT...

AND, AS THE SUN'S *LAST RAYS* ARE SWALLOWED UP BY THE YAWNING EARTH-MOTHER...

...HE COMES AT LAST TO THICK-WALLED *HARAKHT.*

BUT, SOME TIME EARLIER...

NO NEED TO STRUGGLE AND *WRITHE* FETCH-INGLY ANY LONGER, LITTLE BEAUTY.

YOU ARE WELL COME TO *HARAKHT!*

SK-REE!

AND I'LL BE *HAPPY* WHEN I'M WELL *GONE!*

A TRUE *FIRE-BREATHER* OF A WENCH, EH-- AND AT LEAST PART *SHEMITISH*, BY YOUR ACCENT!

WE *LIKE* SHEMITE WOMEN HERE, THOUGH ONLY TO WARM OUR *HEARTHS*, SO--

LET *GO* OF ME, DOG.

I *SAID*--

--LET *GO!*

AUGK

STOP HER! SHE HAS KAMUT'S *KNIFE!*

AND I'LL *SHARE* IT WITH THE FIRST OF YOU TO TAKE A STEP *NEAR* ME!

FOOL! WE HAVE *ARROWS.*

FIRE THEM, THEN, AND BE *DAMNED* TO YOU!

BÊLIT IS NOT AFRAID TO *DIEEEE*❖

YOU *CLUMSY* JACKALS!

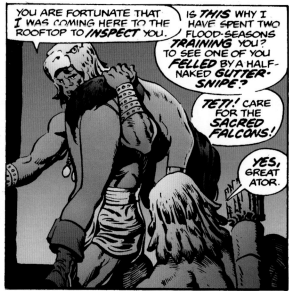

YOU ARE FORTUNATE THAT *I* WAS COMING HERE TO THE ROOFTOP TO *INSPECT* YOU.

IS *THIS* WHY I HAVE SPENT TWO FLOOD-SEASONS *TRAINING* YOU? TO SEE ONE OF YOU *FELLED* BY A HALF-NAKED *GUTTER-SNIPE?*

TETI! CARE FOR THE *SACRED FALCONS!*

YES, GREAT ATOR.

LIKE ONE WHO WALKS UNSCATHED THRU *FLAMES,* THE ONE CALLED *TETI* DOES AS HE'S BADE...

NOR DO THE HUGE PREDATORS SEEM TO *MIND* TRADING THE SKY'S FREEDOM FOR A *FULL GULLET.*

WHILE, WITHIN...

AH, *MONTU!* FOUND A *SLAVE WENCH* ON THE BARGE, DID YOU?

AYE! SHE PRE- FERRED SERVITUDE IN *HARAKHT* TO A SWIMMING BOUT WITH A *CROCODILE.*

OHH--! MY *HEAD*-- IT FEELS AS IF THE *PILLARS OF ISHTAR* FELL UPON IT!

WISEST FOR YOU, BÊLIT, TO ACT AS IF THAT'S *JUST* WHAT HAPPENED.

NEFTHA!? HOW--?

SILENCE!

THIS WAY--!

YOU CANNOT GO BEFORE THE *GREAT KING* SMELLING OF *FALCONS* AND *RIVER-MUD.*

BY THE *HAWK-GOD,* MONTU! THE PAIR HAD DUSKY *DYE* ON THEM THAT WASHES RIGHT *OFF.*

IF *HOR-NEB* DOESN'T WANT ONE I'LL CLAIM HER *MYSELF.*

I'LL PUT A *DAGGER* IN ONE OF US FIRST!

HOW CAN YOU TAKE THIS SO *CALMLY,* NEFTHA?

I WAS *BORN* IN SLAVERY; ONE *ADJUSTS.*

KEEP MOVING -- AND *NO WORDS,* I SAID!

GIVE ME A *BLADE,* DOG, AND YOU'LL BE SAYING *"NO HANDS"* INSTEAD!

HAIL, *HOR-NEB-- GREAT KING* OF *HARAKHT!*

WE, YOUR *HAWK-RIDERS,* BRING YOU THE *LIVING SPOILS* OF OUR *FIRST VICTORY.*

WELL *DONE,* ATOR.

I HAVE *ALREADY* VIEWED THE LESS *NUBILE* PORTIONS OF THE KHEMI MERCHANT'S GOODS...

THIS PART OF OUR FIRST PRIZE, I WOULD REVIEW WITH FAR MORE *LEISURE*.

AYE, YOU'VE DONE *WELL*, ATOR, YOU AND YOUR RIDERS.

THEY ARE BOTH *COMELY* WENCHES-- BUT I RATHER THINK THE ONE WHO WEARS THE SKIN OF *WILD BEASTS* MORE TO MY LIKING.

BÊLIT GRITS HER TEETH, UNSURE WHETHER TO ATTACK NOW, OR LATER--

--WHEN SHE IS SUDDENLY *RELIEVED* OF THAT FATEFUL DECISION:

HALT! THIS MOCKERY MUST *CEASE!*

WHAT?? WHO DARES CRY *"HALT"* IN THE THRONE-CHAMBER OF HOR-NEB!

WHO *WOULD* DARE-- BUT I, *MER-ATH*--

--HIGH PRIEST OF THE HAWK-GOD *HARAKHT*, FOR WHOM THIS CITY IS NAMED!

YOU KNOW *FULL WELL*, HOR-NEB, THAT WE ARE *CO-MONARCHS* OF THIS MIGHTY CITY--

--AND THAT HARAKHT'S *TEMPLE* SHARES ALL SPOILS *EQUALLY* WITH THE *ROYAL TREASURE-ROOM!*

GIVE *ME* THE GIRL WHO WEARS THE SKIN OF WILD BEASTS--FOR, SUCH A ONE WILL MAKE A BETTER *TEMPLE WOMAN* THAN ONE WHO SMELLS OF *PERFUMED SLAVE-HAREMS!*

YOU ARGUE YOUR CASE *WELL*, MER-ATH, FOR A MAN OF THE *GODS.*

BUT, I'VE LONG WANTED A *SHEMITISH* WENCH IN MY *SERAGLIO*--

--AND WHO ARE EVEN *YOU* TO DENY THE WISHES OF THE CITY'S *WARRIOR-KING?*

I AM MER-ATH, *INTERPRETER OF DREAMS*, AMONG OTHER THINGS!

AND I *WANT* THIS WOMAN BECAUSE MY *OWN* NIGHTMARES HAVE SHOWN THE CITY *DESTROYED* BECAUSE OF ONE WHO WEARS THE *SKIN OF ANIMALS*--

--YET ACTS EVERY INCH A *QUEEN!*

BÊLIT *TENSES;* IF THEY KNOW SHE IS THE PIRATE QUEEN OF THE *BLACK COAST*--!

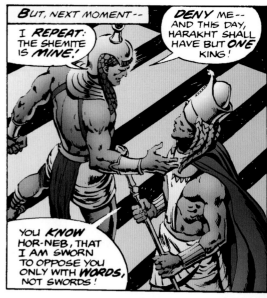

BUT, NEXT MOMENT--

I *REPEAT:* THE SHEMITE IS *MINE!*

DENY ME-- AND THIS DAY, HARAKHT SHALL HAVE BUT *ONE* KING!

YOU *KNOW* HOR-NEB, THAT I AM SWORN TO OPPOSE YOU ONLY WITH *WORDS,* NOT SWORDS!

THEN YOUR OPPOSITION IS *USELESS,* HAVING NO *POINT.*

TAKE THE *OTHER* FOR YOUR TEMPLE WENCH, AND *GO!*

BUT I SHALL HAVE *MUCH* TO SAY, WHEN WE TALK *LATER.*

AS YOU *EVER* DO, MER-ATH.

YOU!

YOU MISERABLE OFFSPRING OF *SPARROWS!* GET YOU *GONE!*

DO YOU THINK I NEED AN *HONOR GUARD*-- AGAINST *ONE* UNARMED GIRL?

PERHAPS YOU *DO,* HOR-NEB.

YOU DARE TO *ADDRESS* ME, WITHOUT *AVERTED EYES?*

WHY SHOULD I BOW-- TO ONE WHO SHARES HIS NARROW THRONE WITH A *PRIEST?*

HE SPEAKS TO YOU AS AN EQUAL.

AND WHY SHOULD HE *NOT?*

FOR, HE IS *MORE* THAN SIMPLY THE *GODS' REPRESENTATIVE* IN THIS CITY.

HE IS ALSO-- MY OWN *BROTHER.*

AND NOW, OUR TIMELINES *CONVERGE* AT LAST...

...AS A STRANGELY *BRONZED* HAWK-RIDER STRIDES MOUNT-LESS, UP TO *HARAKHT'S BARRED GATES...*

...AND PROCEEDS TO TRY THE TACTIC *SUREST* TO GAIN HIM SWIFT ENTRANCE TO THE CITY.

YOU INSIDE! OPEN UP!

WHO IN *SET'S NAME*--?

CONAN'S *STYGIAN* HAS IMPROVED, OVER THE PAST FEW WEEKS.

MY NAME IS... *RASIRITH.*

I WAS ON A MISSION TO *LUXUR,* BUT MY *HAWK* DIED ON ME.

A *MISSION?* WHY DON'T THEY TELL US THESE MATTERS?

ENTER, O HAWK-RIDER!

HOLD! THOSE *BOOTS!* YOU'RE *NO* HAWK-RIDER!

AYE! WE ARE NOT TO *BLAME* FOR--

FOOLS--

NEXT TIME, YOU'LL PAY LESS ATTENTION TO A MAN'S *HEADGEAR--*

--AND MORE TO HIS *ACCENT!*

OR MAYBE I PICKED UP MORE FROM *NEFTHA* THAN I'D *THOUGHT.*

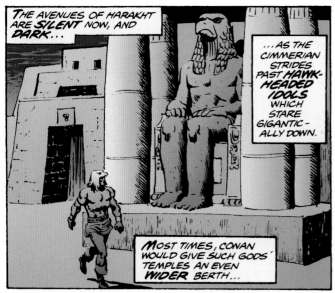

THE AVENUES OF HARAKHT ARE *SILENT* NOW, AND *DARK*...

...AS THE *CIMMERIAN* STRIDES PAST *HAWK-HEADED IDOLS* WHICH STARE GIGANTIC-ALLY DOWN.

MOST TIMES, CONAN WOULD GIVE SUCH GODS' TEMPLES AN EVEN *WIDER* BERTH...

BUT, *TONIGHT* HE MERELY GROWLS TO HIMSELF THAT THE HAWK-GOD WILL HAVE *CORPSES A-PLENTY* TO GAZE DOWN UPON...

...IF ANYTHING HAS HAPPENED TO *BÊLIT!*

WHILE, IN THE VERY *TEMPLE* THAT CONAN SHUNS, IN HIS SEARCH FOR THE *PALACE ROYAL*...

MILORD *MER-ATH,* IF YOU'LL BUT TELL ME MY *DUTIES*...!?

EH? OH--TIME ENOUGH FOR THAT *TOMORROW,* GIRL.

YOU'LL HAVE THE OPPORTUNITY TO LEARN THEM *WELL,* IF LONG LIVES RUN IN YOUR FAMILY.

SOMETHING *TROUBLES* MY LORD.

IS THERE AUGHT THAT *I* CAN--?

IT'S NO *SECRET,* GIRL! IT'S THAT DEVIL *HOR-NEB.*

IN HIS LUST FOR *POWER,* I FEAR HE'LL BRING OUR VERY *CITY* TUMBLING ABOUT OUR HEADS.

I FEAR I DON'T--

YEARS AGO, OUR *MUTUAL* FATHER *KA-MOS* MANAGED TO MAKE HARAKHT LARGELY *INDEPENDENT* OF THE CROWN AT *LUXUR.*

SINCE THAT DAY, WE HIS *SONS* HAVE RIDDEN A *NARROW ROAD:*

TOO *WEAK,* AND WE INVITE *KING CTESPHON* TO TRY TO *REASSERT* LUXUR'S PRIMACY.

TOO *STRONG--* AND WE *FORCE* HIM TO TAKE ACTION, OUT OF *FEAR* OF US!

ALL HAS GONE *WELL* ENOUGH, UNTIL A FEW *MOONS* AGO...

"AT THAT TIME, *HOR-NEB* LED A SCOUTING PARTY INTO THE HILLS-- TO INVESTIGATE A *FALLING STAR* I HAD RIGHTLY NAMED AN *OMEN.*

"HE FOUND THERE *THREE FALCON'S EGGS* -- BUT *ENORMOUS* IN SIZE!

"HE *ALSO* FOUND A STRANGELY-SHAPED *ROCK* WHICH HE TOOK TO BE THE TOPPLED *STAR.*

"HIS GIANT RETAINER *GOL-THIR* HAD BEEN BROUGHT ALONG, TO HELP *CARRY* IT, IF FOUND...

"BUT NOW, THE HANDS OF *MOST* OF THE WARRIORS WERE FULL.

"SOON, THE MIGHTY EGGS *HATCHED...*

"AND THE *GREAT HAWKS* WITHIN HAVE GROWN -- AND *GROWN* -- AND *BRED.*

"NOR HAVE THEY PROVED *HARDER* TO TRAIN THAN *NORMAL* HUNTING-FALCONS...

HOR-NEB KEPT THE *FALLEN STAR*--THE GODS KNOW *WHERE*!

WHAT *AFFRIGHTS ME* IS THAT FOR THE *FIRST TIME* THIS DAY--

--HE USED THE SACRED FALCONS FOR AN ACT OF *RIVER PIRACY*!

WHEN *LUXUR* OR *KHEMI* LEARN OF IT-- THERE SHALL BE *WAR*!

NEED THEY LEARN? NO ONE *ESCAPED* TO TELL THEM.

TRUE, I'LL ADMIT,...

BUT, WHAT HAPPENS WHEN *NEXT* HOR-NEB--?

SET'S SCALES!

A *COMMOTION*-- IN THE *STREETS* BELOW--!

AND, IN THE THRONE ROOM OF *HOR-NEB* HIMSELF--

WHAT IN THE NAME OF THE *SEVEN BEAST-GODS*--?

FOR, ALREADY SHE *KNOWS* WHO ALONE COULD CAUSE SUCH A SUDDEN *UPROAR* IN A CITY WHICH WAS *DEATHLY QUIET* A MOMENT SINCE--

COME *CLOSER*, YOU STYGIAN *DOGS*--!

I'LL GIVE YOU *ALL* A TASTE OF *AKBITANAN STEEL*!

BÉLIT'S SAVAGE HEART LEAPS AT THE SOUND OF *BLOODY STRIFE* FROM THE COURTYARD--

--AND THE *REAL* SIGHT EASILY MATCHES EVEN THE *IMAGINED* ONE !

CONAN! UP HERE, MY LOVER--

UP HERE, AMRA!

WHAT--?

GUARDS! IT SEEMS MY NEW *CHAMBER-WENCH* KNOWS THAT MANGY-HAIRED *RABBLE* IN THE STREET.

TAKE HER IN *HAND*-- TILL HIS CARCASS IS *CARTED AWAY*!

IF THERE ARE ANY *CARCASSES* TO BE HAULED, HOR-NEB--

--THEY'LL BELONG TO YOUR LOW-BORN *LACKEYS*!

OR TO *YOU*, IF I CAN GET MY *BOOT* NEAR YOUR YAPPING *MOUTH*!

GUGGH

THEN, WHILE *ONE* UNEVEN STRUGGLE GOES ON IN THE *PALACE* ITSELF--

--ANOTHER IS GOING ON **BELOW!**

THE MERE **HANDFUL** OF STYGIANS WHO HAVE SURROUNDED THE CIMMER-IAN HAD NO WAY OF **SUSPECTING** IN ADVANCE THAT THEY HAD CORNERED A **WOUNDED LION.**

AND, BY THE TIME HE **STRIKES** SUDDENLY-- HIS **FLASHING KNIFE-BLADE** WEAVING A GLEAMING PAT-TERN LIKE **SUMMER LIGHTNING--**

--IT IS FAR **TOO LATE!**

BUT, THEN, HEARING THE SOUND OF **APPROACHING FOOTSTEPS**, CONAN KNOWS THIS **NEW** GROUPING WILL **NOT** UNDERESTIMATE HIM...

FOR, **THESE** STYGIANS HAVE **SEEN** WHAT ONE LONE WARRIOR HAS DONE TO THEIR **COMRADES--** AND THEY'LL NOT GIVE HIM THE CHANCE TO **REPEAT** THE LESSON.

SURROUND THE INTRUDER-- AND SEND FOR **AH-MIN THE ARCHER.!!**

PERHAPS THEY BELIEVE THAT SO **DEADLY** A FIGHTER WILL POSSESS A **CODE OF HONOR** WHICH WILL PREVENT HIS **FLEEING.**

IF SO, CONAN SWIFTLY **DISABUSES** THEM OF THE NOTION...

HE'S CLIMBING THE WALL LIKE A DAMNED **MONKEY!**

STOP HIM!

YET, EVEN IN HEADLONG FLIGHT--

-- THE BARBARIAN IS STILL A *FOE* TO BEWARE!

LOOK OUT!

GAAAA

AND FLOWER-POTS ARE MADE OF *HARD CLAY* IN THE LAND OF THE *RIVER STYX.*

YOU--*AH-MIN!* IT'S *HIGH TIME* YOU GOT HERE!

BRING *DOWN* THAT *BRONZED DEVIL*-- OR YOU'LL BE BACK IN THE *FOOT-SOLDIERY* BY THE *MORNING SUN!*

AYE!

AH-MIN, BORN IN POVERTY, HAS LABORED LONG AND WELL TO *AVOID* THE HARAKHT INFANTRY...

AND, ONLY THE SLIGHTEST GLINT OF *MOONLIGHT* OFF A METALLIC *ARROWHEAD* ENABLES HIS TARGET TO *MOVE,* JUST AS THE LETHAL SHAFT IS *RELEASED...!*

CROM! WELL, THIS *KNIFE* ISN'T DOING ME MUCH GOOD UP *HERE*--

BEST *SHEATHE* IT WHERE IT *WILL!*

YYYY

THERE'LL BE *NO MARCHING* FOR AH-MIN...NOT *EVER.*

BUT, HIS *ENRAGED COUNTRY-MEN* ALREADY HAVE THEIR MINDS ON *OTHER* THINGS...

HAH! NOW WE'VE *GOT* HIM!

AYE! A MOMENT *MORE,* AND HE'LL RUN *FULL* OUT OF--

--WALL.

CONAN SCARCELY *HEARS* THE HALTING *GASPS* FROM BELOW.

FOR, EVEN AS HIS *FEET* TOUCH THE FAR WALKWAY, HE IS *OFF AND RUNNING* ONCE MORE, LIKE SOME UNKNOWN HYBRID OF RAGING *TIGER* AND LITHE *GAZELLE...!*

STILL, IT WILL TAKE MORE THAN *SWIFT FEET* TO STAY FREE MUCH *LONGER.*

THEN, AS HIS *EYES* DART HERE AND THERE, LIKE THOSE OF A *BEAST AT BAY...*

...HE SEES A SIGHT *ALMOST* TO MAKE HIM BELIEVE IN THE *EFFICACY OF PRAYER:*

A MASSIVE STONE IMAGE OF *HARAKHT,* HAWK-GOD OF *HARAKHT.*

HIS ASTONISHED PURSUERS ARE STILL MILLING ABOUT ON THE *FAR SIDE* OF THE WALL AS HE *LEAPS* BOLDLY DOWN--

--WHERE *OTHER* MEN WOULD PAUSE TO *CONSIDER,* AND REMAIN TO *DIE.*

HIS SHEER *RECKLESSNESS* HAS GIVEN HIM A FEW EXTRA *SECONDS*--

--AND HE MEANS TO *USE* THEM!

CONAN IS NOT ONLY *SWORDLESS* NOW, BUT WHOLLY *WEAPONLESS* AGAINST THE *STYGIAN* SWORDS WHICH ROLL TOWARD THE TEMPLE--

--UNLESS HE CAN *MAKE* A WEAPON OF A HAWK-IDOL WEIGHING *TONS!*

WITHOUT THOUGHT OF THE *POSSIBILITY* OF FAILURE, *CONAN* PUTS HIS STRONG *BACK* AND MIGHTY *SHOULDERS* INTO IT--

--AND HE FEELS IT *MOVE*-- SLIGHTLY, ALMOST IMPERCEPTIBLY.

HIS *HEART* PUMPS BLOOD NEAR TO BURSTING--ALL THE POWER AND FURY OF *23 GRIM YEARS* RADIATE OUTWARD FROM HIS STRAINING *SINEWS*.

HE CAN FEEL THE IDOL *ROCKING* NOW--BACK AND FORTH--

--*BACK* AND *FORTH* AND--

:ARRRH--:

IT IS *NOT* MERELY THE FEAR OF A TOPPLING MASS OF *CARVED STONE* WHICH, A MOMENT LATER, MAKES THE STYGIAN GUARDSMAN *BREAK AND RUN.*

NO, IT WAS ALSO THEIR *GOD* WHO FELL, IN EARTHLY FORM--

--AND THE UN-BELIEVABLE *SIGHT* FILLS THOSE WHO SURVIVE WITH SUDDEN *TERROR!*

BUT THEN, EVEN AS CONAN LOOKS ABOUT FOR A PLACE OF *SAFE-TY--*

HOLD, OUT-LANDER--!

TAKE *ONE STEP* IN ANY DIRECTION-- AND THOUGH I MUCH *ADMIRE* THIS PRETTY THROAT--

--I'LL PLAY A *SHARP MELODY* ON IT!

SHOVE HIS *SWORD* DOWN HIS *THROAT,* MY LOVER!

YET CONAN'S *SHRUGGED SHOULD-ERS* HAVE ALREADY TOLD HER HIS IRRE-VERSIBLE *DECISION...*

SO! MY BROTHER HAS *CAPTURED* THE BARBAROUS FOOL WHO INVADED THE PALACE GROUNDS!

IT WAS A *MINOR* DIVERSION, NOTHING MORE.

WHAT WILL THEY *DO* TO HIM?

YOU *KNEW* HIM, DID YOU? WELL *FOR-GET* HIM, GIRL...

HE WAS AS *ONE DEAD,* THE MOMENT HE ENTERED THE WALLS OF *HARAKHT.*

IF HE'S *BLESS-ED,* HE WILL PROVIDE A DAY'S FEAST FOR THE *SACRED FALCONS.*

COME! WE'VE THINGS TO DO.

SILENTLY, NEFTHA FALLS INTO STEP BEHIND THE PRIEST...

...A FAR MORE *DOCILE* FIGURE THAN THE ONE *BELOW.*

WOMAN, YOUR **OUTCRY** BEFORE REVEALED THAT THIS MAN IS THE ONE CALLED **AMRA**.. WHICH MEANS THAT YOU ARE THE FABLED SHE-PIRATE **BÊLIT**.

THE TALES OF YOUR ATTACK ON **KHEMI**, DAYS PAST, IS ALREADY KNOWN TO US-- THOUGH OUR **COUSINS** THINK YOU WENT BACK OUT TO **SEA**.

SO **KILL** US, THEN, AND HAVE **DONE** WITH IT!

NOT SO **HASTY**, LION-MAN...

WHAT AM I TO **KHEMI**, OR KHEMI TO **ME**, THAT I SHOULD SERVE AS HER **AXE-MAN**?

YOU, WOMAN, MUST HAVE GUESSED THAT I MEAN TO **FREE** THIS CITY OF ALL RULE BUT MY **OWN**.

YOU COULD BECOME A **GREAT FIGURE** IN HARAKHT--IF YOU COULD ADD YOUR **BLACK CORSAIRS** TO MY ARMIES

YOU GO TO HELL.

WHAT OF **YOU**, AMRA? THEY ARE **YOUR** PIRATES, TOO--!

AND IF ONE OF THEM WERE **HERE**, I'D TELL HIM TO SHOVE A **SPEAR** IN YOUR GUT!

ENOUGH BLASPHEMY! TAKE THIS MAN **AWAY**--

--TO THE **PIT OF SHADOWS**!

WELL, MY BLACK-COAST QUEEN? YOU CAN PERHAPS **SAVE** YOUR LOVER'S LIFE, IF YOU'LL ONLY--?

BÊLIT HESITATES. IF SHE TRIES TO BRING HER CORSAIRS **INLAND**, SHE MUST GIVE UP **FOREVER** HER DREAM OF RE-TAKING THE **THRONE OF ASGALUN** WHICH IS RIGHTFULLY HERS.

YET, CONAN IS **FLESH AND BLOOD**, NOT MERE MARBLE.

IN THE **SILENT PALL**, CONAN SENSES HIS MATE **WEAKENING** BEFORE THIS CROWNED **JACKAL**--

AND, BEFORE THE STARTLED GUARDS CAN PREVENT HIM--

--HE PLUNGES **HEADLONG** INTO THE PIT, WHOSE **DARK END** HE CANNOT SEE!

LIKE A *STONE* DROPPED INTO A DEEP AND WINDING WELL, HIS BODY IS *BRUISED* AND *BUFFETED* AS THE BLACK PIT *CURVES* IN ITS LONG DESCENT--

--TILL, WITHOUT WARNING, HE STRIKES *BOTTOM*!

ECHOES DIE WHIMPERING, AS CONAN RISES PAINFULLY TO HIS FEET--TO PERCEIVE A *FAINT* GLOW.

HOW CAN HE KNOW THAT ITS *SOURCE* IS--THE STAR THAT FELL ON STYGIA?

HE KNOWS ONLY THAT ITS *GLOW* STIRS IN HIM VAGUE AND CURIOUS FEELINGS...

THERE'S NO WAY OUT, SO HE DRAWS *NEAR* IT-- THEN WARILY *TOUCHES* IT--

THEN, SUDDENLY

NO!!

WHO THE--?

CROM'S DEVILS!

YOU DARED LAY A HAND UPON THE *SACRED* STONE!

FOR THAT-- YOU *DIE!*

NEXT ISSUE: THE SECRET OF THE STARS!

"Know, O prince, that between the years when the oceans drank Atlantis and the gleaming cities, and the rise of the sons of Aryas, there was an Age undreamed of, when shining kingdoms lay spread across the world like blue mantles beneath the stars.

"Hither came Conan, the Cimmerian, black-haired, sullen-eyed, sword in hand, a thief, a reaver, a slayer, with gigantic melancholies and gigantic mirth, to tread the jeweled thrones of the Earth under his sandaled feet."

—The Nemedian Chronicles.

Stan Lee PRESENTS: CONAN THE BARBARIAN™

WHEN GIANTS WALK THE EARTH!

ONLY MOMENTS AGO, CONAN LEAPED INTO A DARKLY BECKONING PIT, RATHER THAN SERVE AS A HOSTAGE TO THE STYGIAN CITY-KING HOR-NEB.

NOW, BATHED ONLY BY THE EERIE GLOW OF THE FALLEN STAR-STONE, THE SHACKLED CIMMERIAN TURNS-- TO FACE A GREAT, HULKING GIANT--!

CROM'S DEVILS!

YOU DARED LAY A HAND UPON THE SACRED STONE!

FOR THAT-- YOU DIE!

ROY THOMAS & JOHN BUSCEMA
WRITER/EDITOR · ILLUSTRATOR

ERNIE CHAN, INKER

TOM ORZECHOWSKI, letterer
ARCHIE GOODWIN, consulting editor

FEATURING ENTITIES CREATED BY—
ROBERT E. HOWARD

FOR CONAN, A BARBARIAN BORN, A THREAT *PERCEIVED* IS A THREAT *ACTED UPON*--

UHHGG--!

--AND HE DOES NOT MEAN TO WAIT FOR THAT *GARGANTUAN* HAND TO CRUSH HIM TO THE STONE FLOOR WITH ITS SHEER *WEIGHT!*

IN SO FLEETING AN INSTANT THAT HE WOULD CONSIDER HIMSELF TO BE REACTING OUT OF SHEER *INSTINCT*, CONAN WEIGHS HIS CHANCES OF *SURVIVAL* IF HE TAKES A PURELY *DEFENSIVE* STANCE.

--TO *LOCK* THAT MASSIVE BEARDED *HEAD* BENEATH GREAT, POWERFUL *ARMS* WHICH HAVE BARELY THE LENGTH TO *SURROUND* IT!

IN THE SELFSAME INSTANT, HE IS *LEAPING* WITH A MURDEROUS SNARL AT THE MOMENTARILY STUNNED GIANT--

YET, HIS MORE THAN *200 POUNDS* IS HURLED THE NEXT MOMENT BOTH INTO THE *AIR*--

--AND THROUGH IT--

--TO CRASH AGAINST A NETHER WALL!

THEN, WITH PAINFULLY SLOW TREAD, THE BEHEMOTH STALKS TOWARD HIM--

--AND THE GLEAMING *METEOR* WHICH FELL, A FEW MONTHS AGO, FROM OUT OF THE *NIGHTTIME SKY*--

--INTO AN INSTRUMENT OF *IMMINENT DEATH!*

WHILE, IN THE TEMPLE OF THE *HAWK-GOD*...

MILORD *MER-ATH*... IS THERE *NOTHING* YOU CAN DO TO HAVE THE OUTLANDER CONAN *SPARED?*

IT IS MY BROTHER *HOR-NEB* WHO CONCERNS ME...

I'VE *NO NEED* OF TEMPLE SLAVES WHOSE *SINEWS* ARE BURSTING WITH *BESTIAL POWER*, NEFTHA.

LET HIM *DIE* THERE IN THE PALACE.

".. HE AND HIS VILE PLAN TO CREATE AN *ARMY OF GIANT FALCONS* FROM THE *FEW* WE NOW HAVE...

"...TILL, HE HOPES, *ALL STYGIA* WILL BOW THE NECK AND KNEE TO HIM."

BUT *I'M* YOUR SLAVE *NOW*, MILORD.

STILL, IF HE *SUCCEEDS*, THAT WILL MAKE YOU *CO-RULER* OF THIS ANCIENT LAND.

DOES THAT PROSPECT *PLEASE* YOU?

I AM A *PRIEST* OF THE *HAWK-GOD*... NOT A *WARRIOR*, LIKE HE.

YET, THINK OF THE *GOOD* YOU COULD DO STYGIA--WITH YOU, A *MAN OF THE GODS*, SHARING ITS HELM...!

THINK... OF...

SLAVE AND MASTER...

IN SUCH A MOMENT, THE DISTINCTION LOSES ITS MEANING.

MEANWHILE, THE SECOND FEMALE CAPTIVE IN THE CITY IS PROVING DECIDEDLY LESS PASSIVE...

SCALES OF SET--!

YOU COWARDLY, SLINKING DOGS!

YOU SENT MY LOVER TO HIS DEATH DOWN THAT STINKING PIT, AND BY ISHTAR, I'LL--

HALT!

I, HOR-NEB, WARRIOR-KING OF THE HAWK-CITY, COMMAND IT!

LET THE FIGHTING CEASE, IN THE NAME OF THE FALCON GOD!

AT THE KING'S STRIDENT VOICE, THE SOUNDS OF STRUGGLE ALMOST INSTANTLY FADE IN THE ROYAL PALACE.

THE DUSKY-SKINNED MEN STAND FROZEN, AS IF FEARING THE HORRORS OF HELL IF THEY BUT MOVE...

...AND EVEN BÊLIT STOPS HER BATTLING, TO LOOK UP WITH WONDERING EYES...

...AS HOR-NEB DESCENDS FROM THE THRONE.

THAT IS BETTER.

MUCH MORE, WOMAN, AND YOU'D HAVE FORCED ME TO LET THEM KILL YOU.

BUT, NOW THAT THE WILDNESS HAS PASSED FROM YOU, I AM SURE YOU HAVE SEEN THE FOLLY OF YOUR WAYS.

AFTER ALL, I HAVE OFFERED YOU THE QUEEN-SHIP OF HARAKHT IF YOU BUT SUMMON YOUR BLACK PIRATES--

--TO LEAD THEM, BESIDE MY OWN TROOPS, AGAINST THE OTHER CITY-STATES OF STYGIA.

A BARBARIAN MATE IS A CHEAP PRICE TO PAY FOR A CROWN.

THE CHOICE WAS A SIMPLE ONE, IN TRUTH.

THE CHOICE BETWEEN LUXURIANT LIFE...

...AND PAINFUL, IGNOMINIOUS DEATH.

AND, OBVIOUSLY, BY YOUR VERY *INACTION*...

...YOU HAVE MADE THE *WISER* CHOICE.

GUARDS... *RELEASE* HER.

I THINK SHE WILL CAUSE *NO FURTHER* TROUBLE.

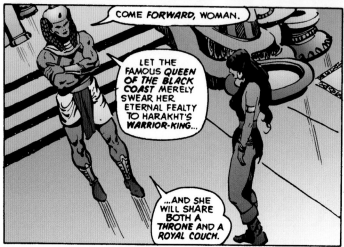

COME *FORWARD*, WOMAN.

LET THE FAMOUS *QUEEN OF THE BLACK COAST* MERELY SWEAR HER ETERNAL FEALTY TO *HARAKHT'S WARRIOR-KING*...

...AND SHE WILL SHARE BOTH A *THRONE* AND A *ROYAL COUCH*.

WELL *?*

YOU SCUM-SUCKING STYGIAN *SWINE*--!

WHAT--?

SEIZE HER!

YOU THOUGHT I'D *JOIN* YOU--BECAUSE YOU HURLED CONAN TO HIS *DOOM?*

BY DERKETA, I'D JOIN HIM IN *HELL* BEFORE I'D SIT BESIDE YOU ON THE *THRONE OF HEAVEN!*

THEN THAT IS *PRECISELY* WHAT YOU *SHALL* DO, YOU SHEMITE WITCH!

TAKE HER AWAY--

--AND LET HER LEARN THE *MEANING* OF A STYGIAN HELL!

MEANWHILE, CONAN-- HIS EYES STARING WIDE AT BOTH TOWERING GIANT AND GLOWING STAR-STONE ABOVE HIM SEEMS ABOUT TO ENTER THE NETHER REALMS ON HIS OWN--

--WHEN SUDDENLY, DESPERATELY, HE TAKES ADVANTAGE OF THE FACT THAT THE MAN-BRUTE'S LONG ARMS GIVE HIS OWN STRONG LEGS ROOM FOR MANEUVER--

--AND, AS THE STRANGELY GLOWING STONE DROPS FROM AN AIR-CLAWING HAND--

--THE HUMAN BEHEMOTH SWIFTLY FOLLOWS IT TO THE HARD STONE FLOOR OF THE SUNKEN CHAMBER!

NOW, GIANT-- I DON'T KNOW WHY THE DEVIL YOU TRIED TO BASH MY SKULL TO A PULP--

BUT, NOW YOU SEEM TO BE HAVING TROUBLE RISING-- LIKE A TURTLE TURNED ON ITS BACKSIDE--

AND, BY CROM, I'LL SPLIT YOU OPEN LIKE ONE, AS WELL!

CONAN HAS SLAIN MANY MEN IN PITCHED COMBAT, AND NEVER BLINKED AN EYE.

WHY, THEN, DOES HE HESITATE THIS TIME...

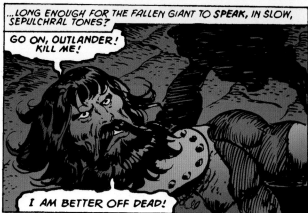

...LONG ENOUGH FOR THE FALLEN GIANT TO SPEAK, IN SLOW, SEPULCHRAL TONES?

GO ON, OUTLANDER! KILL ME!

I AM BETTER OFF DEAD!

WELL?

GO AHEAD!!

NO!

PERHAPS I AM FAIR GAME FOR THE *MAD-HOUSE*--BUT, MITRA HELP ME, YOU PIQUE MY *CURIOSITY*, GIANT!

RISE, AND TELL ME WHAT MAKES THIS STUPID *PIECE OF ROCK* WORTH KILLING FOR.

IT WOULDN'T BRING *TWO DRAKIS* IN THE BAZAARS OF *SHADIZAR* THE WICKED!

DID YOU *HEAR* ME, GIANT?

I SAID *RISE!*

SIMPLE WORDS TO *SAY*--BUT *NOT* A SIMPLE THING FOR *GOL-THIR* TO DO--

--NOT SINCE HE BECAME THE *KEEPER OF THE SACRED STONE.*

I'VE GROWN-- TOO *BIG!*

YOU MEAN--YOU WEREN'T *ALWAYS* THIS SIZE?

ONLY A FEW *MOONS* GONE, I WAS NO LARGER THAN *YOU*--WHICH STILL MADE ME THEN *CHIEF* AND STRONGEST OF *HOR-NEB'S* PERSONAL GUARDSMEN.

THEN, WE FOUND YONDER *TOPPLED STAR*--

--AND THE *EGGS!*

EGGS?! WHAT KIND OF *GIBBERISH* ARE YOU TALKING *NOW?*

LOOK IN HERE-- AND YOU SHALL *SEE!*

ALL RIGHT-- BUT, IF THIS IS A *TRICK*--!

I WAS BEATEN *FAIRLY*--AND I WILL NOT *RENEW* THE STRUGGLE.

I WAS A *WARRIOR* BEFORE I BECAME... A *FREAK.*

BEHOLD! IT IS FROM *HUGE EGGS* SUCH AS *THOSE,* THAT--

--THAT HARAKHT'S *GIANT FALCONS* WERE HATCHED! OF COURSE!

THAT THING YOU CALL THE *SACRED STONE*--THAT *"STAR"* WHICH FELL FROM THE *SKY*--

--MUST SOMEHOW CAUSE *LIVING* THINGS TO *GROW!*

STILL, ITS *MAGIC* MUST WORK ON *UNBORN* CREATURES DIFFERENTLY THAN ON *YOU.*

FOR, THE GREAT HAWKS FLY *HIGH,* WHILE YOU HAVE TROUBLE MERELY *STANDING UPRIGHT!*

WELL, IT'S NOT MY CONCERN.

I JUST WANT *OUT!*

YOU *SPARED* ME--THUS, EVEN THOUGH I'LL BE HAPPIER WHEN I'VE *DIED,* I'LL HELP YOU *ESCAPE,* IF I CAN--

--IF YOU'LL *VOW* NOT TO *HARM* MY *MASTER HOR-NEB,* WHO MUST HAVE HAD YOU *CAST* HERE.

YOU'VE *GUESSED* HE'S NOT ONE OF MY *FAVORITES,* EH?

WELL, I *VOW* TO *TRY* TO AVOID KILLING HIM--IS THAT *SUFFICIENT?*

AYE.

THIS *CREVICE* MIGHT LEAD TO ESCAPE; I DO NOT *KNOW* WHERE IT GOES.

AND I *WON'T* MEAN TO *FIND* OUT!

I'LL *CLIMB* BACK OUT THE WAY I *CAME.*

IMPOSSIBLE! THE *TUNNEL* IS LONG--CURVED-- JAGGED--!

I'LL MANAGE.

THIS NECK-CHAIN WON'T HELP MUCH, THOUGH.

HERE, OUTLANDER! LET *ME!*

YOU'RE *STRONG* BEYOND *WORDS*--EVEN THOUGH THE *EARTH* PULLS YOU *MERCILESSLY* DOWN!

WHY DON'T YOU *LEAVE* THIS PLACE-- WALK IN THE *SUN* AMONG *MEN* AGAIN?

NAY! EVEN IF THE KING LET ME, MEN WOULD STRIVE TO *DESTROY* ME OUT OF *FEAR!*

YOU'RE... DOUBTLESS *RIGHT.*

FARE YOU *WELL,* GOL-THIR.

I *HOPE* WE MEET *AGAIN* ONE DAY.

THEN, TOWARD THE *LIGHT* FROM ABOVE CONAN MAKES HIS *LONG,* TORTUROUS *ASCENT*-- USING ARMS AND LEGS AND BACK TO AN EXTENT SCARCELY *IMAGINABLE* TO A MODERN-DAY MAN...

AND ALL THE WHILE, HE THINKS OF HIS MATE BÊLIT IN THE TENDER CLUTCHES OF HOR-NEB, HALF-KING OF HARAKHT...

...AND HE HATES HIMSELF FOR GIVING HIS WORD TO GOL-THIR.

LOVE AND HATRED:

BETWEEN THE TWO OF THEM, THEY SUSTAIN THE BATTLE-WEARY CIMMER-IAN DURING HIS ARDUOUS, PAINFUL CLIMB...

...TILL, AT LAST, HE HAULS HIS ACHING BODY INTO A THANKFULLY EMPTY THRONE-CHAMBER.

IT IS NIGHT NOW, AND ONLY A SINGLE SHAFT OF MOONLIGHT MAKES THIS CHAMBER BRIGHTER THAN THE ONE HE LEFT BELOW.

THEN, EVEN AS HIS EYES SWIFTLY ADJUST TO THE DIM LIGHT, HE SEES AN OPEN DOORWAY WHICH IS THE ONLY EGRESS FROM THE ROOM.

WARILY AS A TIMBER WOLF SNIFFING AT A SUSPECTED TRAP, CONAN MOVES TO AND THROUGH THE DOORWAY.

NOR, DESPITE HIS MORE THAN TWO HUNDRED POUNDS, DID ANY WOLF OR PANTHER EVER MOVE MORE SILENTLY IN UNFAMILIAR SURROUNDINGS.

IT IS PITCH BLACK WITHIN THE NEXT CHAMBER -- A MOST UNNATURAL DARKNESS. FOR SURELY THERE SHOULD BE A DOOR OR WINDOW SOMEWHERE, IF ONLY TO SERVE AS --

THEN, WITHOUT WARNING --

CROM!

--MYRIAD TORCHES FLARE BLINDINGLY, THRUST THROUGH PREVIOUSLY UNSEEN APERTURES--

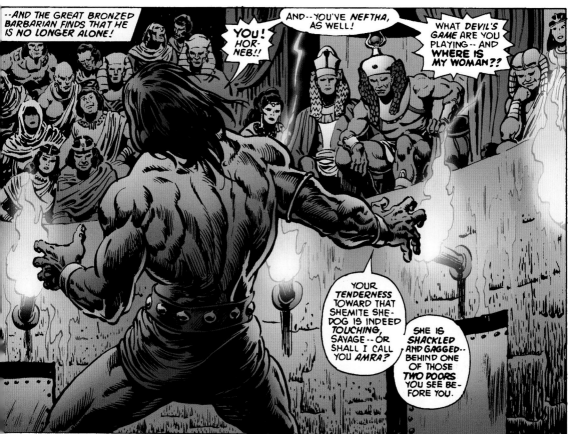

--AND THE GREAT BRONZED BARBARIAN FINDS THAT HE IS NO LONGER ALONE!

AND--YOU'VE *NEFTHA,* AS WELL!

YOU! HOR-NEB!!

WHAT *DEVIL'S GAME* ARE YOU PLAYING -- AND *WHERE IS MY WOMAN??*

YOUR *TENDERNESS* TOWARD THAT *SHEMITE SHE-DOG* IS INDEED *TOUCHING,* SAVAGE -- OR SHALL I CALL YOU *AMRA?*

SHE IS *SHACKLED* AND *GAGGED* -- BEHIND ONE OF THOSE *TWO DOORS* YOU SEE BE-FORE YOU.

WHY DO YOU *PLAY* THESE SENSE-LESS, CRUEL GAMES, HOR-NEB?

SILENCE, BROTHER! LET THE *PRIEST-KING* NOT DISPUTE THE *WARRIOR-KING!*

BEHIND *ONE DOOR,* SAVAGE, IS YOUR SO-CALLED *MATE...* PER-HAPS EVEN *FREEDOM.*

BEHIND THE *OTHER* -- *DEATH,* WITH SHARP CLAWS!

WELL? AFFORD US A MOMENT'S AMUSEMENT, LION OF THE SOUTH!

CHOOSE -- BEFORE I ORDER MY MEN TO SLAY YOU WHERE YOU STAND!

CHOOSE? AYE, I'LL CHOOSE ALL RIGHT, STYGIAN --

BUT I CHOOSE *NO* DOOR!

I CHOOSE *YOU* -- YOUR *NECK,* BENEATH MY FINGERS!!

FORGOTTEN NOW, IN THE HEAT AND FRENZY OF THE MOMENT, IS ANY VOW MADE TO A *CRIPPLED GIANT* -- FOR, CONAN SEES THAT THE WALLS ARE *LOW,* BY CIMMERIAN STANDARDS --

--LOW ENOUGH TO BE **SCALED** IN A FEW SHORT **SECONDS**--

--IF HE CAN FIND BUT THE MEREST **HANDHOLD!**

BUT, **HOR-NEB** OBVIOUSLY HAS **HEARD** OF CIMMERIAN PROWESS AT CLIMBING--FOR, THE WALLS HAVE BEEN **NEWLY GREASED**--

--AND NOT EVEN A **HILL-MAN** CAN FIND HANDHOLDS WHERE **NONE EXIST!**

DAMN!

CONAN IS **UP** ALMOST INSTANTLY; HE'LL WASTE **NO** MORE TIME IN FUTILE EFFORTS TO **ESCAPE.**

BUT, WHICH DOOR TO CHOOSE--WHEN THE ANSWER MEANS **LIFE,** BOTH FOR HIMSELF AND FOR THE **WOMAN HE LOVES??**

HE HESITATES...

AND, AS HE DOES, HIS DARTING EYES FASTEN UPON THE SLAVE GIRL **NEFTHA,** SEATED BESIDE **MER-ATH...**

...VERY **CLOSE** BESIDE.

I CANNOT STAND THE **SUSPENSE,** DEAR **MER-ATH!** PLEASE TELL ME-- **WHICH DOOR?**

WHY? WAS THAT ROGUE **YOUR** LOVER AS WELL AS THE **SHEMITE'S?**

WHAT COULD SUCH AS **HE** MEAN, TO ONE WHO WAS A SERVANT IN THE **PALACE** AT LUXUR?

I JUST... WANT TO KNOW...!

HOR-NEB HIMSELF HAS TOLD ME.

THE DOOR ON HIS **LEFT** IS THE SAFE ONE.

I **THANK** YOU, MILORD. I COULD NO LONGER TAKE THE **STRAIN...!**

AS SHE SPEAKS, SHE GESTURES SLIGHTLY...

...TOWARD THE DOOR ON CONAN'S LEFT!

DARING NOT EVEN TO THINK THAT NEFTHA MAY WISH HIM **DEAD** FOR SOME UNKNOWN REASON, HE ADVANCES TO THE INDICATED DOOR...

...AND PUSHES IT **OPEN.**

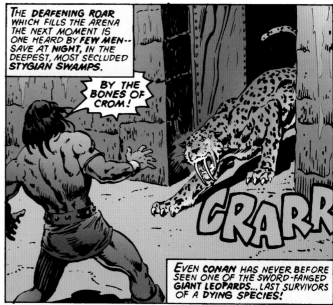

THE **DEAFENING ROAR** WHICH FILLS THE ARENA THE NEXT MOMENT IS ONE HEARD BY **FEW MEN--** SAVE AT **NIGHT,** IN THE DEEPEST, MOST SECLUDED **STYGIAN SWAMPS.**

BY THE BONES OF CROM!

CRARR

EVEN **CONAN** HAS NEVER BEFORE SEEN ONE OF THE **SWORD-FANGED GIANT LEOPARDS...** LAST SURVIVORS OF A DYING **SPECIES!**

MER-ATH! YOU **LIED** TO ME!

NAY! I BUT TOLD YOU--

--WHAT **I** TOLD HIM, WOMAN!

I **KNEW** A VIXEN LIKE YOU COULD WORM THE SECRET FROM MY WEAK **BROTHER,** AND THUS **WARN** THE BARBARIAN--

SO, I TOLD HIM THE **WRONG DOOR--** AND LET **NATURE** TAKE ITS PROPER COURSE!

GUARDSMAN! TAKE HER **AWAY--** TILL THE DRAMA **BELOW** BE FINISHED, AND SHE CAN BE **DISPOSED OF!**

YES, MAJESTY!

THE GUARDSMAN IS USED TO **PLIANT** WOMEN, SUCH AS THOSE WHO MIND THE HEARTHS OF **HARAKHT...** AND SURELY, THE PALE-

...UP TILL THE INSTANT WHEN SHE SUDDENLY GRASPS HIS **SHEATHED SWORD--**

SCALES OF SET--!

--AND USES IT TO HURL **HIM,** HIS EYES STILL OPEN WIDE FROM SHEER **SURPRISE--**

--INTO THE ARENA WHERE **DEATH** SPORTS SIX-INCH CANINES!

FOR, EVEN A **GIANT BEAST** OF PREY WILL USUALLY CHOOSE WHAT SEEMS THE **EASIEST** QUARRY.

RRRHFF!

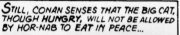

STILL, CONAN SENSES THAT THE BIG CAT, THOUGH **HUNGRY**, WILL NOT BE ALLOWED BY HOR-NAB TO EAT IN PEACE...

AND THEN, **HE** WILL BE THE **ONLY** MOVING THING FOR THE CARNIVORE TO **ATTACK!**

JUST THEN--

CONAN! HERE!

YOU'RE MORE OF A WOMAN THAN I **THOUGHT**, NEFTHA!

NOW TO SEE IF **THIS** DOOR REALLY--

BÊLIT!

Uhhhn..!

WHAT--IS **HAPPENING,** MY LOVER? I FEEL-- **WEAK--!**

YOU'VE BEEN **LOTUS-DRUGGED!** THAT DEVIL HOR-NEB WILL **PAY,** IF I CAN GET **NEAR** H--

NOW WHAT'S GOING ON OUT THERE??

AT THE **FAR END** OF THE ARENA, A PREVIOUSLY-UNNOTICED **IRON PANEL** SLIDES UPWARD--TO REVEAL A **LOOMING, SHADOWED SHAPE** WITHIN!

NEXT MOMENT, SHARP SPEARS PROD HIS LUMBERING, UNSTEADY FRAME INTO THE CIRCLE...

GO ON, GIANT!

YOU KNOW WHAT WE TOLD YOU-- AND WHAT YOU MUST DO!

YES...!

GOL-THIR! SO! THEY'LL MAKE US FIGHT, WE WHO HAVE MORE IN COMMON WITH EACH OTHER THAN THOSE WE'VE SERVED!

WELL, GOL-THIR? I'M TOLD YOUR STRENGTH MATCHES YOUR NEW SIZE.

USE IT-- TO KILL FOR YOUR KING, ONE WHO TRIED TO KILL ME!

DON'T, MAN! YES, I BROKE MY VOW-- BUT ONLY TO SAVE MYSELF AND MY WOMAN!

I DON'T WANT TO HAVE TO RUN YOU THRU--!

THE BARBARIAN KNOWS WELL HOW TO READ THE THOUGHTS OF MEN FROM THEIR EYES.

HE SEES NOW THAT THIS GIANT--SO POWERFUL, YET SWAYING SO UNSTEADILY ON LEGS NEVER MEANT TO HOLD HIS MASS--HAS EYES FILLED WITH UNRELENTING HATE.

BUT--HATE FOR WHOM?

THEN, WITH A BURST OF SPEED WHICH CATCHES CONAN BY SURPRISE, A MAMMOTH HAND SHOOTS OUT--TO CLOSE LIKE AN IRON CLAMP ON HIS UPPER ARM!

OWWW! WHAT--?

EVEN NOW, THE GIANT IS FALLING--HIS LEGBONES SNAPPING LIKE GRAVITY'S TWIGS--

YET, HIS ARMS ARE STILL MIGHTY--

--MIGHTY ENOUGH, WITH ONE LAST EFFORT, TO LIFT THE BURLY CIMMERIAN BODILY INTO THE AIR--

-- AND HURL HIM WHERE *ANIMAL GREASE* WILL DO NO GOOD!

FOR THE *LIFE* OF ME, I CAN'T GUESS *WHY* GOL-THIR CHOSE TO *HELP* ME--

--BUT I'LL NOT LOOK TOO CLOSELY AT A *GIFT-STALLION'S* TEETH!

GUARDS! GUARDS!

AND THE *GUARDS* COME--

--TOO MANY OF THEM TO BE HELD BACK FOR LONG BY ANY SWORDSMAN!

THEN, CONAN SPIES AN *OPENING* -- A CLEAR PATH FOR HIS *SWORD*, IF NOT FOR HIMSELF, TO THE *AMBITION-MAD* HOR-NEB--

--AND HE *TAKES* IT!

YOU *DOGS* CAN *GUT* ME--

--BUT YOU'LL DO SO FOR A *DEAD KING!*

YET, IN HIS *FEAR*, HOR-NEB HAS *STAGGERED* JUST FAR ENOUGH THAT HE IS MERELY STRUCK PAINFULLY IN THE *ARM.*

IT IS SUFFICIENT, ALL THE SAME.

AS HE *TOPPLES DOWNWARD*, STILL TOO STUNNED EVEN TO CRY OUT--

--ONTO THE *MOTTLED BACK* OF *DOOM!*

RRRR

FIRST, HOR-NEB IS AWARE OF A RINGING IN HIS EARS--THE RESULT OF THE FALL.

THEN, **ABOVE** THE RINGING, A **ROARING** WHICH GROWS LOUDER, **LOUDER**--

--TILL IT FILLS HIS **EARS**--

--AS ITS **MAKER** FILLS HIS SIGHT--

--AND **DROWNS** OUT EVEN HIS **DEATH-SCREAM!**

IT ALL HAPPENS TOO QUICKLY FOR THE GUARDS TO **PREVENT.**

BUT, THERE IS STILL... REVENGE.

MER-ATH! SPARE HIM--FOR MY SAKE!

YOU **BETRAYED** MY TRUST ONCE! **STILL**--

--I **DETEST** VIOLENCE, AND THE USE OF **BRUTE FORCE!**

MY BROTHER BROUGHT HIS FATE UPON **HIMSELF**--AND I AM **SOLE KING** NOW IN HARAKHT.

GUARDS-MEN! LOWER YOUR SPEARS!

RRRR

BÊLIT!?

STILL UNDER THE INFLUENCE OF THE **LOTUS**, THE SHE-PIRATE HAS WAN-DERED FROM RELATIVE **SAFETY** INTO THE **CENTER** OF THE BLOODIED ARENA...

AND NOW, UNABLE TO **STAND** OR EVEN TO **SEE**, SHE IS NEARER TO **DEATH** THAN SHE HAS BEEN IN **MANY A MOON!**

THE GUARD'S HAND IS STRONG-- THE HAND THAT *TEARS* THE SPEAR FROM HIS GRASP, STRONGER BY *FAR!*

GIVE ME THAT!

YOU!

CAT!

THE SHOUT *ECHOES* THRU THE CHAMBER--

--ACCOMPLISHING ITS DESPERATE PURPOSE!

THE LONG-FANG *TURNS* TOWARD THE BRONZED CREATURE THAT *THREATENS* IT--

BUT, ITS *FIRST* LEAP AT THE MAN WHO WAS ITS *ORIGINAL* INTENDED VICTIM...

...IS LIKEWISE ITS *LAST!*

CONAN IS AT BÊLIT'S *SIDE* EVEN WHILE THE DYING BEAST STILL *TWITCHES* CONVULSIVELY NEARBY...

ARE YOU--?

I AM... NOW!

IN THE *STANDS* ABOVE, LOYAL GUARDSMEN NOW HAIL HIM WHO WEARS THE CROWN OF BOTH PRIEST *AND* WARRIOR KING...

...A MAN WHO *LOATHES* VIOLENCE, AND WAR WAGED BY GIANT FALCONS...

...A MAN WHO OWES HIS THRONE IN PART TO THE *SLAVE* GIRL WHO SMILES HER ENIGMATIC SMILE AT HIS *SIDE.*

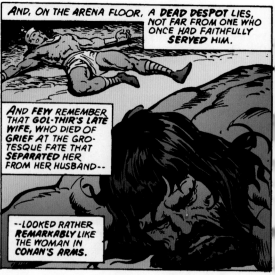

AND, ON THE ARENA FLOOR, A *DEAD DESPOT* LIES, NOT FAR FROM ONE WHO ONCE HAD FAITHFULLY *SERVED* HIM.

AND *FEW* REMEMBER THAT GOL-THIR'S *LATE* WIFE, WHO DIED OF *GRIEF* AT THE GROTESQUE FATE THAT *SEPARATED* HER FROM HER HUSBAND--

--LOOKED RATHER *REMARKABLY* LIKE THE WOMAN IN CONAN'S ARMS.

NEXT: **ON TO LUXUR-- AND THOTH-AMON!**

"Know, O prince, that between the years when the oceans drank Atlantis and the gleaming cities, and the rise of the sons of Aryas, there was an Age undreamed of, when shining kingdoms lay spread across the world like blue mantles beneath the stars.

"Hither came Conan, the Cimmerian, black-haired, sullen-eyed, sword in hand, a thief, a reaver, a slayer, with gigantic melancholies and gigantic mirth, to tread the jeweled thrones of the Earth under his sandaled feet."

—The Nemedian Chronicles.

STAN LEE PRESENTS: CONAN THE BARBARIAN ™

THE LOST VALLEY OF ISKANDER!

THE DAYS JUST PAST HAVE BEEN *HARD, WEARY* ONES FOR CONAN, BÉLIT, AND THE SLAVE-GIRL NEFTHA ON THEIR WAY TO *LUXUR,* CAPITAL OF SERPENT-RIDDLED *STYGIA.*

DRAGONS FROM THE SEA— *GREAT HAWKS* WHICH CARRIED *MEN* THRU THE SKIES— *DOOMED GIANTS* WITH MUSCLES OF STEEL— ALL THESE HAS THE BRONZED CIMMERIAN FACED AND FOUGHT!

YET, THE DEAD-LIEST, MOST DREADED FOE OF *EVERY* MAN IS THE LOOMING SPECTRE CALLED *TIME*—!

ROY THOMAS, HOWARD CHAYKIN, ERNIE CHAN
WRITER/EDITOR   GUEST-ARTIST TEAM

JOHN COSTANZA, ARCHIE GOODWIN
letterer   CONSULTING EDITOR

FREELY ADAPTED FROM THE STORY by *ROBERT E. HOWARD* CREATOR OF CONAN

IT IS THE STEALTHY SCRAPE OF A *LEATHERED HEEL ON STONE* THAT AWAKENS CONAN.

INSTANTLY, HE KNOWS THAT THE SOUND COMES FROM OFF TO HIS *RIGHT* AND *ABOVE*.

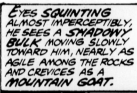

EYES SQUINTING ALMOST IMPERCEPTIBLY, HE SEES A *SHADOWY BULK* MOVING SLOWLY TOWARD HIM, NEARLY AS AGILE AMONG THE ROCKS AND CREVICES AS A *MOUNTAIN GOAT.*

HE *RESISTS* THE TEMPTATION TO LEAP TO HIS FEET--FOR, THE WOULD-BE ASSASSIN IS STILL OUT OF *SWORD RANGE.*

BUT *THEN,* WHEN THAT DUSKY FIGURE *LOOMS* ABOVE HIM IN THE DIM STARLIGHT--

--A CURVED *STYGIAN KNIFE* RAISED HIGH AND AIMED FOR HIS *HEART*--

--CONAN SUDDENLY GOES INTO ACTION LIKE A *STEEL SPRING* UNCOILING!

FANGS OF SET.!!

YOU SKULKING DOG!

ONE HAND *CHECKS* THE DESCENDING WRIST, AS SURELY AS IF IT WERE AN UN-YIELDING *STONE WALL*--

--AS, *SIMULTANEOUSLY,* HE HEAVES *UPWARD* AND LOCKS THE *OTHER* SAVAGELY ON A *HAIRY THROAT!*

URRKK--!

AFTER HIS INITIAL *OUTBURST OF ANGER,* CONAN FIGHTS AS EVER IN *GRIM SILENCE.*

NOR DOES ANOTHER SOUND COME FROM THE STRAINING LIPS OF THE *MAN BENEATH.*

DUSKY HANDS TEAR FUTILELY AT THE WRIST WHOSE *IRON FINGERS* TIGHTEN VISE-LIKE, MOMENT BY MOMENT--

THEN, WITH A CONVULSIVE *SHUDDER,* THE STYGIAN ASSAILANT'S BODY GOES *LIMP.*

AND, AS THE *LIFELESS CORPSE* SLUMPS LIKE A DISCARDED DOLL TO THE GROUND, CONAN *SEES* FOR THE FIRST TIME THE *FACE* OF HIS ATTACKER:

AK-NER! THE VERY MAN WHOM *MER-ATH* SENT ALONG TO *GUIDE* HIM!

AT THAT REALIZATION, CONAN INSTINCTIVELY FEELS UNDER HIS *BELT...* DRAWING FORTH FROM A *POUCH* THERE A STRANGE *ROUND JEWEL.*

IT LOOKS NOT UNLIKE A GREAT *STARING EYE*-- AND SO IT *IS:*

THE *EYE* OF *SET!*

SUDDENLY, CONAN'S *KEEN EARS* TELL HIM THAT *OTHER MEN* ARE PROWLING ABOUT HIM, OUT THERE AMONG THE ROCKS...

HE CANNOT *SEE* THEM, AND HE KNOWS THEY CANNOT SEE *HIM* AMONG THE CLUSTERED BOULDERS HE HAD CHOSEN FOR HIS *SLEEPING SITE.*

BUT THEY ARE THERE!

THOUGH, EVEN SO, HE CANNOT STOP HIS *AGILE MIND* FROM RACING *BACK* A FEW SHORT DAYS--

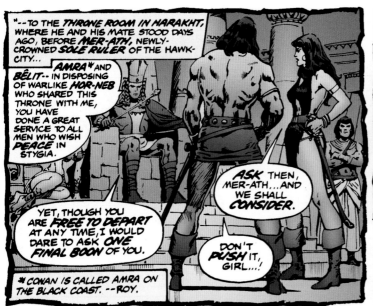

"--TO THE *THRONE ROOM IN HARAKHT*, WHERE HE AND HIS MATE STOOD DAYS AGO, BEFORE *MER-ATH*, NEWLY-CROWNED *SOLE RULER* OF THE HAWK-CITY...

*AMRA** AND *BÊLIT*-- IN DISPOSING OF WARLIKE *HOR-NEB* WHO SHARED THIS THRONE WITH ME, YOU HAVE DONE A GREAT SERVICE TO ALL MEN WHO WISH *PEACE* IN STYGIA.

ASK THEN, MER-ATH...AND WE SHALL *CONSIDER*.

YET, THOUGH YOU ARE *FREE TO DEPART* AT ANY TIME, I WOULD DARE TO ASK *ONE FINAL BOON* OF YOU.

DON'T *PUSH* IT, GIRL....!

* CONAN IS CALLED AMRA ON THE BLACK COAST. --ROY.

THIS IS AN *EYE OF SET*-- ONE OF A *PAIR OF GREAT GEMS* WHICH ARE HOLY TO US OF HARAKHT.

FOR MANY YEARS, OUR CITY HAS *KEPT PEACE* WITH A CERTAIN *VILLAGE* IN THE SOUTHERN HILLS WHICH IS CALLED *ATTALUS*...

...BY *EXCHANGING* ONE EYE-JEWEL FOR *ANOTHER*, WHICH ATTALUS POSSESSES, WHEREVER A *NEW MONARCH* TAKES THE THRONE OF EITHER PLACE.

WE ASK *YOU*, AMRA, TO BE THIS TIME THE *LONE WARRIOR* WHO MAKES THE JOURNEY SOUTHWARD...

IN RETURN, WE PROMISE YOU *SAFE PASSAGE TO LUXUR*, SO THAT YOU MAY FULFILL WHATEVER *UNSPOKEN MISSION* YOU HAVE THERE.

WE *ASK* THIS BOON BECAUSE IT IS WRITTEN THAT THE *STRONGEST* AND *BRAVEST* MAN IN THE CITY SHOULD BE THE ONE TO *CARRY* IT.

WILL YOU *DO* IT?

WELL... I...

HOLD!

WHO--?

HUN-YA-DI! WHAT WISHES MY *SUCCESSOR* AS HIGH PRIEST?

AS THE NEW HIGH PRIEST, I FEEL IT IS *I* WHO SHOULD CHOOSE THE MAN TO CONVEY THE *EYE OF SET* TO ATTALUS ...RATHER THAN *YOU*, O' KING.

I AM *SORRY*, HUN-YA-DI, BUT IT MUST BE *MY* DECISION.

NOW, AMRA... YOU WERE *SAYING*...?

I WILL TAKE THE JEWEL TO THIS VILLAGE, MER-ATH... IN EXCHANGE FOR *SAFE PASSAGE* ON MY RETURN.

DONE! HUN-YA-DI WILL GIVE YOU *DIRECTIONS*... AND A MAN TO *GUIDE* YOU!

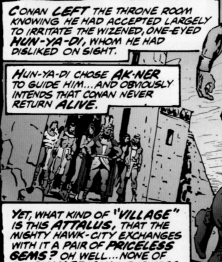

CONAN *LEFT* THE THRONE ROOM KNOWING HE HAD ACCEPTED LARGELY TO IRRITATE THE WIZENED, ONE-EYED *HUN-YA-DI*, WHOM HE HAD DISLIKED ON SIGHT.

HUN-YA-DI CHOSE *AK-NER* TO GUIDE HIM... AND OBVIOUSLY INTENDS THAT CONAN NEVER RETURN *ALIVE*.

YET, WHAT KIND OF "VILLAGE" IS THIS *ATTALUS*, THAT THE MIGHTY HAWK-CITY EXCHANGES WITH IT A PAIR OF *PRICELESS* GEMS? OH WELL...NONE OF THE *CIMMERIAN'S* BUSINESS...

CONAN **SEES** NOW, IN HIS MIND'S VISION, WHAT THE ONE-EYED PRIESTLING **HUN-YA-DI** WISHES:

TO GAIN ONE OF THE TWO **EYES OF SET**, AND USE IT TO ESTABLISH HIS CLAIM TO BE **CO-RULER OF HARAKHT** WITH THE NEWLY-CROWNED **MER-ATH!**

A FEW MORE AFTER **THAT**, THERE WOULD BE BUT **ONE** KING AGAIN-- AND IT WOULD **NOT** BE MER-ATH.

CONAN HIMSELF CARES LITTLE **WHO** RULES THE HAWK-CITY-- BUT HE HAS SWORN TO **MER-ATH** TO REACH HIDDEN **ATTALUS** WITH HIS BURDEN.

HE'S BEEN **BOUGHT** AND **PAID FOR**, IN A **SENSE**, BY THE PROMISE OF SAFE PASSAGE TO **LUXUR** AND THE COURT OF THE FEARFUL **KING CTESPHON**.

AND CONAN TENDS TO **STAY** BOUGHT.

SUDDENLY, A **HUMAN PRESENCE** IN THE PITCH-BLACK SHADOWS BRINGS HIM BACK TO THE WORLD OF **REALITY**...

FA-TAH! IS THAT **YOU**? IS THE DOG **DEAD**?

WHY DID YOU NOT CALL MEE EEEE

CONAN STRIKES **UNERRINGLY** IN THE DIRECTION OF THOSE HOARSE **STYGIAN** ACCENTS.

HE FEELS HIS SWORD **BITE FLESH**-- HEARS THE SOFT, SAD SOUND OF A **MAN** CRUMPLING, LIFELESS, TO THE **ROCKY FLOOR**...!

KILL HIM! THE OUTLANDER MUST **DIE!!**

THEN, ALL ABOUT CONAN THERE RISES A SUDDEN CLAMOR OF VOICES--THE RASP OF **BOOTED FEET** ON ROCK--

--AND THE DEADLY SWISH OF **ARROWS,** FIRED IN STARLIT DARKNESS!

CASTING STEALTH TO THE **WINDS,** THE BARBARIAN SPEEDS OFF DOWN THE JAGGED **SLOPE**--

--WHILE, BEHIND HIM, THERE SOUNDS A STRIDENT **CHORUS OF YELLS** NOW, AS THE MEN IN HIDING **GLIMPSE** HIS BRONZED FIGURE FOR A MOMENT--

--ONLY TO SEE IT **SWALLOWED UP** IN SHADOWY GULFS!

NOR ARE HARAKHT'S ARCHERS TRAINED TO FIGHT AT **NIGHT.**

HE **LAUGHS** INWARDLY AS HE THINKS OF THEM **RAVING,** TO HIS REAR, LIKE **FOILED WOLVES** IN THEIR BEWILDERED **RAGE!**

THEY'LL BE **AFTER** HIM, AYE--BUT WITH THE **START** HE HAS--!

THEN, SUDDENLY THE **EARTH** GAPES BLACKLY, EMPTILY **BEFORE** HIM--

--AND NOT ALL HIS STEEL-TRAP **QUICKNESS** CAN SAVE HIM AS HIS GRASPING HANDS CATCH ONLY **THIN AIR**--

--AND HE PLUMMETS INTO A **RAVINE,** HIDDEN THERE UNSUSPECTED AMONG THE SHADOWS WHERE THE STARSHINE CANNOT GO.

ARRR

A **SOFTER** SKULL THAN A **CIMMERIAN'S** WOULD DOUBTLESS HAVE BEEN **SPLIT OPEN** LIKE A RANCID EGG.

AS IT IS, HE LIES VERY, VERY **STILL**....FOR A LONG **TIME.**

A CHILL *DAWN* IS WHITEN-ING THE SKY WHEN HE *REGAINS* HIS SENSES.

SITTING UP GROGGILY, HE FEELS HIS *HEAD*...WHERE A LARGE *LUMP* IS CLOTTED WITH DRIED BLOOD.

HE KNOWS IT IS ONLY BY *CHANCE* THAT HIS *NECK* WAS NOT BROKEN IN THE FALL.

YET, IF HE HAS LOST *PRECIOUS HOURS*, AT LEAST NEITHER DID HIS *PUR-SUERS* DIS-COVER HIM, UNCONSCIOUS IN THIS HIDDEN RAVINE.

STILL, BY CROM, HE'LL HAVE *WORDS* FOR MER-ATH WHEN HE RETURNS TO THE HAWK-CITY!

IF HE *RETURNS!*

THIS WAS TO HAVE BEEN A MISSION OF *PEACE* -- NOT OF *DEATH*, STEALING UP ON YOU IN THE STAR-STREWN NIGHT!

THE *ARROWS* START FLYING EVEN AS HE REACHES THE *TOP*.

DAMN!

TO THE *SOUTH* SHOWS THE MOUTH OF A *NARROW GORGE*, WALLED BY GREAT *ROCKY CLIFFS* --!

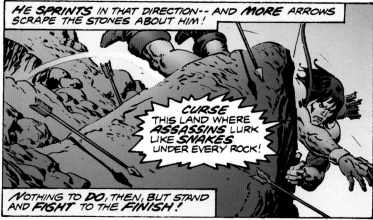

HE *SPRINTS* IN THAT DIRECTION -- AND *MORE* ARROWS SCRAPE THE STONES ABOUT HIM!

CURSE THIS LAND WHERE *ASSASSINS* LURK LIKE *SNAKES* UNDER EVERY ROCK!

NOTHING TO *DO*, THEN, BUT STAND AND *FIGHT* TO THE *FINISH!*

YET, A FEELING OF *FUTILITY* TUGS AT HIS HEART, EVEN AS HE FITS AN *ARROW* TO HIS *STYGIAN* *BOW*...

FOR, HE CAN SCARCELY HOPE TO ESCAPE *ALL* THE BLOODTHIRSTING MEN WHO CHASE HIM -- NOT *NOW*, IN BROAD *DAYLIGHT!*

STILL, HIS SHARP EYES *PEER* CLOSELY AT THE SKY-THRUSTING *BOULDERS* ABOVE HIM -- AND, WHEN A *FIGURE* SHOWS THERE FOR A BRIEF INSTANT --

-- HE PROVES HOW **WELL** HE LEARNED HIS LESSONS, A FEW YEARS BACK, IN THE **TURANIAN ARMY!**

GGAAAR

IT IS A **HEAVY** STYGIAN WHO SCREAMS AND **TOPPLES FORWARD** --

-- AND THE **IMPACT** OF HIS HURTLING BODY **DISLODGES A BOULDER** FROM ITS UNSTABLE BASE!

IT ROLLS DOWN THE SLOPE ALONG WITH THE **BODY,** DISPLACING OTHERS AS IT GOES --

-- TILL, BARELY **AUDIBLE** ABOVE THE ROAR OF LETHAL, CASCADING **ROCK** --

-- CAN BE HEARD ONE OF THE MOST **DREAD** CRIES OF ANY HILL- COUNTRY:

AVALANCHE!

EVEN AMID THE DIN, CONAN **RECOGNIZES** THE VOICE:

HUN-YA-DI, THE MAN WHO WOULD BE **PRIEST-KING!**

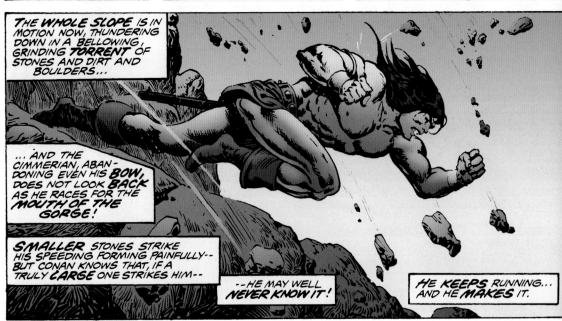

THE **WHOLE SLOPE** IS IN MOTION NOW, THUNDERING DOWN IN A BELLOWING, GRINDING **TORRENT** OF STONES AND DIRT AND BOULDERS...

... AND THE **CIMMERIAN,** ABANDONING EVEN HIS **BOW,** DOES NOT LOOK **BACK** AS HE RACES FOR THE **MOUTH OF THE GORGE!**

SMALLER STONES STRIKE HIS SPEEDING FORMING PAINFULLY-- BUT SPEEDING CONAN KNOWS THAT, IF A TRULY **LARGE** ONE STRIKES HIM--

-- HE MAY WELL **NEVER KNOW IT!**

HE **KEEPS** RUNNING... AND HE **MAKES** IT.

THOSE WHO SERVE *HUN-YA-DI* ARE LESS *FORTUNATE*.

CROUCHING IN THE *PROTECTING* SHADOW OF A *GREAT ROCK*, CONAN CAN *HEAR*, ABOVE THE ROARING, THE *AWFUL SCREAMS* THAT MARK THE *END OF MEN'S LIVES*--

--MEN CAUGHT AND CRUSHED AND GROUND TO BLOODY SHREDS UNDER THE RUSHING TONS OF *SHALE* AND *STONE*!

YET, EVEN AS HE WATCHES, THE BARBARIAN KNOWS THAT ONLY A *TRICKLE* OF THE AVALANCHE HAS BEEN DIVERTED INTO THE *GORGE*.

THE *MAIN BULK* OF IT THUNDERS ON *DOWN THE MOUNTAIN*.

PERHAPS THIS SIGHT IS WHY CONAN CANNOT BELIEVE, AS SO MANY DO, IN THE *VENGEFUL RETRIBUTION* OF *ANGRY GODS*.

WHAT *AROUSED DEITY* COULD BE MORE *FEARSOME* THAN THE *EARTH ITSELF*, WHEN AFFRONTED BY THE *LEADEN*, TRESPASSING FEET OF *MEN*?

AT LENGTH, AN *UNEARTHLY SILENCE* FOLLOWS IN THE WAKE OF THE LANDSLIDE'S *ROAR.*

HERE AND THERE PROTRUDE *GRISLY REMINDERS* THAT THE MOUNTAIN HAS CLAIMED A *SACRIFICE.*

OF *HUN-YA-DI* AND ANY OTHER SURVIVORS, THERE IS NO *SIGN.*

THEN *WHY* IS CONAN SO *CERTAIN* THAT THE AMBITIOUS PRIESTLING *DID* SURVIVE?

HE COULD NOT *SAY,* IN TRUTH... BUT HE'S HAD SUCH HUNCHES *BEFORE.*

THEY'VE PROVED MORE OFTEN *RIGHT* THAN *WRONG.*

WELL THEN, *LET* HUN-YA-DI REGROUP... PERHAPS EVEN RECRUIT *NEW* STYGIAN HILL-PEOPLE TO *SUPPORT* HIS LOFTY CLAIMS!

RIGHT NOW... BRUISED, HALF-DAZED, BEREFT OF BOW... CONAN IS HAUNTED BY A MORE *IM-MEDIATE* THREAT:

STARVATION.

MER-ATH SAID GAME WAS *SCARCE* IN THE PEAKS SOUTH OF HARAKHT.

THE GORGE IS STILL TWISTING AND BENDING BETWEEN *TORTUOUS WALLS,* WHEN, WITHOUT WARNING--

SLAY ME!

MITRA'S CROWN!

SLAY ME AND *HAVE DONE* WITH IT, YOU *SERPENT-WORSHIPPING DOG!*

YOU'LL NOT HEAR *BARDYLIS* BEG FOR *SET'S MERCY!*

WHOA NOW! JUST **SLOW DOWN** A MOMENT, GIRL!

I'M **NO** SNAKE-KISSER!

LIE STILL, AND I'LL **HELP** YOU--IF I CAN.

CAN'T-- GET MY **LEG--** OUT FROM BENEATH THIS **STONE--!**

IS YOUR LEG **BROKEN?**

I--I THINK **NOT!** BUT IF YOU ROLL THE BOULDER EITHER WAY IT WILL **GRIND** MY LEG TO **SHREDS!**

YOU'RE **RIGHT THERE!**

THEN, I'LL HAVE TO **LIFT** IT-- --UNNH!--**STRAIGHT UP!**

ARE YOU **MAD?**

PTOLEMY HIMSELF COULD SCARCELY LIFT IT-- AND **YOU** ARE NOT NEARLY SO **LARGE** AS HE!

CONAN DOES NOT STOP TO INQUIRE WHO **PTOLEMY** MAY BE... OR TO EXPLAIN THAT STRENGTH IS **NOT** ALTOGETHER A MATTER OF **SIZE ALONE.**

NOW, HIS **HEELS** DIGGING INTO THE DIRT, THE **VEINS** IN HIS TEMPLES SWELLING, HE **GRIPS** THE STONE--**STRAINS MIGHTILY**--

UHHHHNNN

--AND **LIFTS** IT!

NNN!

ONLY A **FLEETING MOMENT** IS THE HUGE STONE IN THE AIR-- BEFORE, OF NECESSITY, **GRAVITY** PULLS IT IRRESISTIBLY **DOWN** AGAIN...

BUT, IN THAT MOMENT, THE GIRL HAS **ROLLED FREE!**

AND CONAN IS STILL **PANTING,** SHAKING THE **PERSPIRATION** FROM OFF HIS CRAGGY FACE...

...BEFORE THE YOUNG FEMALE'S *GRATITUDE* IS MADE *UN'MISTAKABLY CLEAR.*

I AM *BARDYLIS.*

I AM *CONAN,* A CIMMERIAN... AND I WANT *NO ONE'S* LIFE.

MY *LIFE* IS YOURS.

I'VE *ENOUGH* TO TAKE CARE OF WITH MY *OWN.*

BUT WHO *ARE* YOU? YOU'RE TOO *PALE* TO HAVE BEEN WITH *HUN-YA-DI'S* KILLERS.

I WAS *HUNTING* ON THE CLIFFS WHEN THE AVALANCHE STRUCK.

COME TO MY *VILLAGE,* AND WE SHALL-- AI!'EEEE! *LOOK OUT!*

WHAT THE *DEVIL--?*

CONAN *WHEELS--*

--EVEN AS, HIGH UP THE BEETLING *GORGE* WALL, A *DUSKY FORM* LETS FLY A WHISTLING *ARROW!*

WHETHER HUN-YA-DI LIVES OR NOT, SOME OF HIS *MEN*-- AND THUS HIS UNHOLY *MISSION*-- DECIDEDLY *DO!*

*B*UT CONAN AND THE GIRL WILL *NOT,* IF THEY PAUSE TO *RUMINATE.*

THIS *WAY!*

THE GIRL *LIMPS* SLIGHTLY, INSOFAR AS SHE IS NOT FULLY *PROPELLED* BY CONAN'S *FORWARD THRUST--*

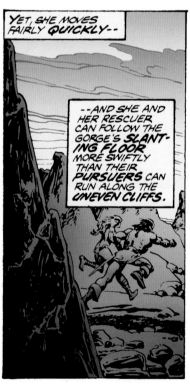

*Y*ET, SHE MOVES FAIRLY *QUICKLY*--

--AND SHE AND HER RESCUER CAN FOLLOW THE GORGE'S *SLANTING* FLOOR MORE SWIFTLY THAN THEIR *PURSUERS* CAN RUN ALONG THE *UNEVEN* CLIFFS.

*M*INUTES LATER, *EMERGING* FROM THE FURTHER MOUTH OF THE GORGE--

OUR RESPITE WILL BE *BRIEF!* HUN-YA-DI'S *JACKALS* WILL SOON BE ON US AND--

CROM'S DEVILS! WHAT'S *THAT??*

WHY--

--THAT'S MY VILLAGE!

THREE HUNDRED FEET DOWN THE SHEER CLIFF, CONAN SEES A DEEP VALLEY, HEMMED IN ON ALL SIDES BY GIGANTIC PRECIPICES... A STREAM WINDING AMONG DENSE TREES, FAR BELOW THE NARROW TRAIL ON WHICH THEY STAND.

FURTHER ON, CONAN SEES WHAT SEEM TO BE STONE BUILDINGS REARED AMONG THOSE DARK-GREEN GROOVES... AND KNOWS AT ONCE THAT HE HAS FOUND THE PLACE HE HAS SOUGHT!

WE CAN'T STAY ON THIS TRAIL; THEY'LL BE ON US AND SHOOT US LIKE RATS.

I COULD PERHAPS CLIMB DOWN THE CLIFF, BUT I CAN'T LEAVE YOU HERE TO--

IT IS A SECRET WAY, AND NONE BUT A MAN OF MY PEOPLE HAS EVER FOLLOWED IT... AND THEN ONLY WHEN HARD PRESSED.

YOU DON'T HAVE TO!

I JUST REMEMBERED-- THERE ARE HAND-HOLDS CUT INTO THE ROCK, AT THIS VERY POINT!

CAN YOU MAKE IT WITHOUT FALLING?

CONAN GRUNTS.

SINCE WHEN DO PALE BLONDE GIRLS QUESTION CIMMERIANS ABOUT SCALING MOUNTAINS?

YET, NEXT INSTANT, WITH *BARDYLIS* TO GUIDE HIM, HE BEGINS A *PERIL-DESCENT...*

...AND CONAN *MARVELS* THAT THE GIRL IS NEARLY AS AGILE AS *HE.*

CRANING HIS NECK UPWARD, CONAN SEES A *BEARDED FACE* PEERING MALEVOLENTLY DOWN AT HIM...AS A *DUSKY HAND* DRAWS AN *ARROW* FROM A QUIVER!

DAMN!

...AS THEY CLING LIKE *FLIES* TO THE STONE WALL, FINDING THE SMALL, MAN-MADE *NICHES* WHICH PIT THE ROCK...

HE FINDS HIM-SELF *EAGER* NOW, RATHER THAN MERELY *ANXIOUS,* TO REACH THE SO-CALLED *LOST VALLEY.*

AND, IF *ALL* THE WOMEN THERE ARE AS FAIR AS THIS *BARDYL-IS--!*

OUTLANDER! ABOVE YOU!!

SECONDS BEFORE THE CIMMERIAN *AVOIDED* A CER-TAIN *LOOSE STONE* NEAR HIS RIGHT HAND, LEST IT SEND HIM *PLUMMETING* THE LAST SHORT DISTANCE...

NOW, HE *GRASPS* IT WITH A FIERCENESS BORN OF SUDDEN *DESPERATION*--

--TEARS IT FROM ITS PLACE IN THE *SHEER ROCK WALL*--

--AND *FLINGS* IT UPWARD, WITH A SINGLE *SAVAGE* MOTION--

--THE *RECOIL* OF WHICH NEARLY SENDS HIM HURT-LING *BACKWARD* INTO SPACE!

STILL, HIS *AIM* IS AS *TRUE* AS IT WAS *HASTY*--

AAA

--AND A *WRITHING, LIFELESS BODY* STRIKES THE EARTH WITH A SICKENING CONCUSSION AT THE SAME MOMENT CONAN'S FEET ALIGHT ON SOLID GROUND.

BY *CROM!* I'M LUCKY THE MISBEGOTTEN DOG DIDN'T LAND ON *ME!*

OUT--LANDER! YOU ARE *ALL RIGHT*--?

THANKS TO *YOU*, BARDYLIS -- AND *THANKS* FOR THE WARNING SHOUT!

YOU'RE A GIRL AFTER MY OWN *HEART*, IF ONLY I WEREN'T--

WEREN'T *WHAT?*

CONAN REALIZES, SUDDENLY, THAT HE IS *UNCERTAIN* JUST WHAT HE HAD INTENDED TO *SAY.*

BÊLIT IS HIS--*WHAT?*

NEVER MIND.

NOW, TELL ME ABOUT YOUR *"VILLAGE,"* WHILE WE SEEK SHELTER IN THE *TREES.*

WE ARE THE DESCENDANTS OF A *GREAT CONQUEROR*, WHOSE NAME HAS COME DOWN TO US AS *ISKANDER*.

WE DO NOT KNOW *WHENCE* HE CAME, OR *WHEN*-- ONLY THAT *LEGENDS* SAY HE ENTERED THIS VALLEY THRU A *STRANGE BLUE MIST*, LONG AND LONG AGO.

ISKANDER AND HIS ARMY BUILT THE CITY WE CALL *ATTALUS*, AND THEN MARCHED *EASTWARD* AGAIN.

THE EERIE MIST *VANISHED* THEN... AND THOSE SOLDIERS AND THEIR WOMEN *LEFT BEHIND* SOON CAME TO KNOW THEY WERE STRAND-ED FOREVER IN A *WORLD* OR EVEN *TIME* WHICH WAS *NOT THEIR OWN!*

WE *WAIT* FOR HIM HERE... WAIT FOR THE DAY OF *ISKANDER'S RETURN*... AND MANY TIMES HAVE WE *SLAUGHTERED* THE STYGIAN JACKALS WHO CAME *AGAINST* US!

ONLY WITH THE HAWK-CITY *HARAKHT*, WHICH WISHES LIKE US TO BE LEFT ALONE, DO WE LIVE IN *PEACE*-- EXCHANGING CERTAIN *TOKENS* WHENEVER *NEW RULERS* COME TO POWER...!

THUS SPEAKS *BARDYLIS*... NOR CAN SHE KNOW THAT THE NAME *"ISKANDER"* IS BUT ANOTHER FORM OF THE NAME OF A MAN WHOM A FAR-LATER WORLD WILL KNOW AS...

ALEXANDER THE GREAT!

HOW HE JOURNEYED *BACKWARD IN TIME* THRU THE AZURE MISTS WILL DOUBTLESS *NEVER* BE *KNOWN*... YET, COME HE *DID*...

...TO *CONQUER* AND TO FOUND A *GRECIAN DYNASTY* WHICH NOW RULES THIS LOST VALLEY IN AN AGE NEARLY *10,000* YEARS BEFORE HE WILL BE *BORN!*

OF COURSE WE SPEAK *STYGIAN* FOR PURPOSES OF *TRADE*...

BUT, *NO MERCHANT* WE HAVE EVER MET SPEAKS OUR *NATIVE TONGUE.*

THIS IS THE FIRST TIME ANY BUT A *CAPTIVE* OR A *TRADER* HAS ENTERED THE VALLEY IN *CENTURIES.*

SAY NOTHING TILL I *BID* YOU, LEST MY PEOPLE THINK YOU AN *ENEMY.*

FAIR ENOUGH! BUT I MUST SEE YOUR *LEADER* AT ONCE!

WHY? YOU DID NOT SAY *BEFORE*--

WE HARDLY HAD *TIME,* DID WE?

I'M ON A MISSION FOR *MER-ATH,* NEW-CROWNED KING OF *HARAKHT.*

THEN THEY'VE BROUGHT... ONE OF THE *EYES!?*

COULD BE.

BY THE WAY, DO YOU KNOW YOUR *CITY WALL* IS BADLY IN NEED OF *REPAIR?*

NO HOSTILE FORCE HAS EVER *REACHED* THE WALL -- FOR WE GUARD THE *NARROW PASS* AT VALLEY'S END, AS WELL AS THE *HANDPATH* DOWN WHICH WE CLIMBED.

THIS IS OUR *PALACE,* OUT- LANDER.

CONAN.

CONAN THEN.

WITHIN, THEY FILE PAST SOLDIERS WHO WEAR AN UNFAMILIAR ARMOR...

PTOLEMY, KING OF THE VALLEY OF *ISKANDER*--

--I BRING A *FRIEND* OF *ATTALUS,* ONE WHO IS *EMIS- SARY* OF *HARAKHT!*

CONAN'S EYE- BROWS ARCH, HOW- EVER SLIGHTLY...

FOR, THE MAN ON THE THRONE IS A GREAT BLOND GIANT -- NOT SO TALL AS THE STYGIAN GOL-THIRD, YET OBVIOUSLY AS POWERFUL -- AND MUCH MORE IN COMMAND OF HIS STRONG LIMBS, BECAUSE HE HAS POSSESSED THEM FROM BIRTH!

HE SAVED MY *LIFE* FROM STYGIAN ATTACKERS... AND HE COMES IN *PEACE.*

I SHALL DECIDE THAT, *BARDYLIS!*

AND IF I DECIDE HE IS *LYING*--

--HE SHALL *HORRIBLY DIE!!*

NEXT ISSUE: *TRIAL BY FEAR!*

125

"Know, O prince, that between the years when the oceans drank Atlantis and the gleaming cities, and the rise of the sons of Aryas, there was an Age undreamed of, when shining kingdoms lay spread across the world like blue mantles beneath the stars.

"Hither came Conan, the Cimmerian, black-haired, sullen-eyed, sword in hand, a thief, a reaver, a slayer, with gigantic melancholies and gigantic mirth, to tread the jeweled thrones of the Earth under his sandaled feet."

—The Nemedian Chronicles.

Stan Lee PRESENTS: CONAN THE BARBARIAN™

ROY THOMAS WRITER/EDITOR ★ HOWARD CHAYKIN & ERNIE CHAN ILLUSTRATORS ★ DENISE WOHL LETTERER ★ A. GOODWIN CONSULTING EDITOR

TRIAL BY COMBAT!

FREELY ADAPTED FROM THE STORY "THE VALLEY OF ISKANDER" by Robert E. Howard CREATOR OF CONAN.

THE STORY SO FAR: CONAN HAS BEEN SENT BY THE NEW KING OF HARAKHT TO THE STRANGE LOST VALLEY OF ISKANDER, SOMEWHERE IN THE RUGGED HILLS OF STYGIA.

YET, HIS STAY MAY BE SHORT --AND BLOODY--!

GREAT PTOLEMY --I BRING A FRIEND OF OUR CITY ATTALUS --AN EMISSARY FROM THE HAWK-CITY!

HE SAVED MY LIFE FROM STYGIAN DOGS --AND HE COMES IN PEACE.

I SHALL DECIDE THAT, BARDYLIS --AND IF I DECIDE HE IS LYING--

--HE SHALL HORRIBLY DIE!

HE IS **NO** ENEMY, GREAT PTOLEMY!

HE LIFTED A **GREAT STONE** OFF ME -- MORE MASSIVE THAN EVEN **YOU** COULD HAVE --

THAT WE SHALL **SEE** -- WHEN WE SHALL **SEE** IT!

I AM HERE ON A MISSION FROM THE **NEW RULER** OF HARAKHT, GOLD-HAIR...

...NOT TO ENGAGE IN A USELESS **CONTEST OF STRENGTH!**

PLEASE, OUTLANDER-- LET **ME** HANDLE THIS!

HE HAS TRAVELED FAR AND **FOUGHT** FOR US, GREAT PTOLEMY -- AND NOW HE WOULD **FEAST** AND REST.

CAN HE NOT SPEAK **LATER** WITH YOU OF HIS **MISSION?**

AYE, FAIR **ENOUGH,** GIRL!

BUT, IF HE IS A **STYGIAN SPY** -- YOUR HEAD SHALL **ANSWER** FOR IT!

NOW **GO!**

THEN, AS THE CIMMERIAN AND THE WOMAN DESCENDED FROM ALEXANDRIAN GREEKS PUSH THEIR WAY OUT THROUGH THE CROWD WHICH HAS CURIOUSLY GATHERED AROUND THE PALACE...

DO NOT **MIND** PTOLEMY, CONAN. HE IS SHORT OF **PATIENCE** AND SCANT OF **COURTESY.** HE --

WAIT! WHO IS **THAT** MAN -- IN THE GARB OF A **DESERT-DWELLER?**

THAT? IT IS ONLY **ABLAH,** A TRADER WHOM WE ALLOW TO ENTER THE VALLEY WITH **BEADS** AND TRINKETS AND SUCH.

WE TRADE ORE AND WINE AND SKINS FOR THEM. **WHY?**

I... THOUGHT I *RECOGNIZED* HIM... FROM AN EVEN *LESS* HAPPY TIME.

BUT, *NO MATTER.*

LET *US* GO.

THIS IS THE *HOUSE OF MY FATHER,* OUTLANDER.

HE IS A *FINE MAN...* PERDICCAS BY NAME.

WITHIN THE HOUSE, CONAN MARVELS SLIGHTLY AT A WAY OF LIFE SO DIFFERENT FROM HIS OWN...

...AND IN THEIR OWN LACK OF INTEREST IN A WORLD OUTSIDE THE VALLEY OF ISKANDER.

YET, THE MAN *ISKANDER* -- THE GREAT *CONQUEROR* WHO FOUNDED THIS *PLACE* --

--SURELY *HIS* WANDER-LUST WAS AS GREAT AS MY *OWN.*

IT AUGURS *WELL* FOR ME THAT A MAN CAN TRAVEL THE WORLD FOR YEARS AND STILL BE A *KING* IN HIS TIME.

AND WHY SHOULD WE *WISH* TO KNOW OF POINTS *NORTH* OF HERE, CONAN?

WE SHALL NEVER *GO* THERE.

AND *YOU* SAY THAT *NO MAN* OF ATTALUS HAS EVEN BEEN MORE THAN A *DAY'S JOURNEY* FROM THIS *VALLEY!*

STILL, EVEN MIGHTY-THEWED BARBARIANS GET WEARY... AND, WHEN THE GIRL SHOWS HIM HIS SLEEPING CHAMBER...

I DON'T *LIKE* THIS MUCH, BARDYLIS.

THERE'S *NO* DOOR-- ONLY A *CURTAIN*--!

YOU ARE *SAFE* IN THE HOUSE OF *PERDIC-CAS!*

YES... I SUPPOSE I *AM*-- HERE, IF *ANY-WHERE* IN ATTALUS!

GOOD NIGHT, THEN.

AS SOON AS THE GIRL HAS LEFT, CONAN TAKES FROM A HIDDEN POUCH THE GREAT JEWEL WITH WHICH HE HAS BEEN ENTRUSTED --

ONE OF THE TWO EYES OF SET-- ITS MATE IN THE POSSESSION OF THE ATTALANS.

ON THE MORROW, HE WILL EXCHANGE ONE EYE FOR ANOTHER-- AND THERE WILL BE MORE YEARS OF PEACE BETWEEN ATTALUS AND THE HAWK-CITY CALLED HARAKHT.

BUT, FOR NOW, BETTER TO HIDE IT BEHIND ONE OF THE SMALL STONE BLOCKS WHICH COMPOSE THE WALL.

THEN, STRETCHING HIMSELF OUT, HE FALLS TO MAKING PLANS FOR HIS *SAFE RETURN* TO THE CITY WHERE *BÊLIT* AWAITS HIM.

BUT, *WINE* AND *WEARINESS* TAKE THEIR TOLL... AND CONAN'S MEDITATIONS MERGE AT LAST INTO *DREAM.*

THOUGH SAFE IN THIS *VALLEY,* HE KNOWS THAT THE ONE-EYED PRIEST *HUN-YA-DI* LURKS OUTSIDE WITH THE PATIENCE OF A STYGIAN COBRA.

HUN-YA-DI WANTS AN *EYE OF SET,* TO SOLIDIFY HIS CLAIM TO *RULERSHIP* IN HARAKHT--AND HE'LL STOP AT *NOTHING* TO GET IT!

HE SLEEPS *DEEPLY...* AND *LONG.*

AND, WHEN HE *AWAKES,* IT IS IN *UTTER DARKNESS--!*

YET, EVEN IN THE NIGHT, HE HAS HEARD THE SOFT SWISH OF A *CURTAIN* OVER THE DOORWAY...

BARDYLIS-- IS THAT *YOU?*

CONAN'S HAD GIRLS SLIP INTO HIS ROOM *BEFORE*-- YET, EVEN AS HE SPEAKS --

-- HE KNOWS THE *TREAD* HE HEARS IS TOO *HEAVY* TO BE THAT OF THE LITHE-LIMBED *GIRL!*

BUT, EVEN IN THAT MOMENT OF *REALIZATION,* SOMETHING *CRASHES DOWN* UPON HIS HEAD--

AARRGH

-- AND A *DEEPER BLACKNESS* SHOT WITH FIRE-SPARKS ENGULFS HIM!

THE GLOW OF A *TORCH* DAZZLES HIS EYES WHEN HE *AWAKENS.*

STILL, HE RECOGNIZES THE *NON-ATTALAN* AMONG THE FOUR MEN WHO STAND OVER HIS TIGHTLY-BOUND FORM...

SO! HERE LIES THE DREADED *AMRA!*

MY NAME IS *CONAN,* DOG.

AYE -- EVERYWHERE BUT ON THE *BLACK COAST,* WHERE YOU ARE CALLED *"AMRA, THE LION"* --

-- AND WHERE YOU AND THE SHE-DEMON *BÊLIT* ARE THE *MOST FEARED PIRATES* SINCE AHMAAN THE GREAT!

SENSING THAT HIS *ARMS* BUT NOT HIS *LEGS* ARE BOUND HERE IN THIS BARE STONE CHAMBER, CONAN STALLS FOR TIME WHILE HIS *STRENGTH* RETURNS TO HIM...

I *REMEMBER* YOU NOW-- FROM SHADY DEALINGS I HEARD OF IN *ARGOS.* BUT, YOU'VE *NO FEUD* WITH ME.

AH, BUT *OTHERS* HAVE-- OTHERS SUCH AS *HUN-YA-DI,* FOR IN-STANCE.

I *ENCOUNTERED* HIS PARTY WHEN I *LEFT* THE VALLEY TODAY-- AND, SINCE HE HIMSELF CANNOT ENTER IT WITHOUT CAUSING A *BLOODBATH,* HE WILL PAY ME WELL TO BRING HIM THE *EYE OF SET.*

WHERE *IS* IT?

IF I *GAVE* IT TO YOU, I'D STILL NOT LEAVE THIS ROOM *ALIVE.*

I FEAR MY ARRANGEMENT WITH HUN-YA-DI MAKES THAT *IMPOSSIBLE.*

THE *RULERS OF KHEMI* WILL PAY ME BETTER FOR YOUR HEAD THAN *YOU* COULD EVER HOPE TO.

THE ONLY THING YOU CAN *BUY* WITH THE EYE-JEWEL IS A *PAINLESS DEATH.*

THAT IS *NOT,* HOWEVER, A THING TO BE TOSSED AWAY *LIGHTLY!*

YOU GO TO THE *DEVIL!*

HAVE IT YOUR *OWN* WAY, THEN.

CERTAINLY *PTOLEMY* WILL NOT CARE IF YOU DIE-- FOR, IT IS AN *OLD TRADITION* THAT THE KING OF ATTALUS MUST BE THE *STRONGEST MAN* IN THE CITY.

HE WOULD HAVE BEEN FORCED TO KILL YOU *HIMSELF,* IN TIME.

WELL? HAVE YOU *SEARCH-ED* HIM?

WE'VE FOUND *NOTHING,* ABLAH.

BAH! YOU DO NOT KNOW *HOW* TO SEARCH AN OUT-LANDER! *I* WILL DO IT.

CUT HIM LOOSE AND *HOLD* HIM, SO I MAY SEARCH HIS *ARM-PITS!*

NOW, I SHALL-- BY THE FANGS OF SET!

HOLD HIM, YOU FOOLS!

YOU HOLD ME, ABLAH!

GNN GH!

-- STARTING WITH MY *BOOT!*

AS FOR THESE DIM-WITTED *ATTALAN JACKALS* OF YOURS--

--THEY'VE MORE MUSCLES IN THEIR *HEADS* THAN IN THEIR *ARMS!*

ARRRHH--!

G-*GET* HIM, YOU *YELLOW-HAIRED SWINE!*

YOU'VE BEEN *WELL PAID*-- NOW *EARN* YOUR KEEP!

WE SHALL, ABLAH-- *NEVER* FEAR!

SO-- YOU'RE *BOUGHT* AND *PAID* FOR, EH?

WELL, NOTHING WRONG IN *THAT,* I SELL MY *OWN* SWORD AND RIGHT ARM, WHEN-EVER I *CAN!*

BUT THE *NEME-DIAN SKEPTICS* TELL ME THERE ARE FEW PLACES TO SPEND YOUR GOLD--

--IN *HELL!*

NEXT MOMENT, A *GRASPING HAND* LUNGES AT THE EMBATTLED CIMMERIAN--A HAND FULLY AS LARGE AS HIS OWN.

YET, THE HAND WHICH *LOCKS* IT IN A *STEELY GRIP* IS TO THAT HAND--

--AS THE *STRONG WIND* IS TO THE *WILLOW-REED* IT *SNAPS!*

HRRK!

TEETH-BARED, CONAN TURNS TO THE *REMAINING OF THREE ATTALANS*--

WELL? DO YOU WANT TO *SHARE* YOUR BROTHERS' FATE?

IT'S CERTAIN THAT *ABLAH* ISN'T GOING TO BLOODY HIS HANDS TRYING TO *HELP* YOU.

I'LL BLOODY MY *OWN* HANDS, OUTLAND PIG!

BLADES, EH?

WELL, IT WAS A *WARRIOR* FROM ANOTHER TIME AND PLACE WHO *FOUNDED* THIS STRANGE CITY--

WE'LL SOON SEE IF HIS *DESCENDANTS* ARE ALSO HEIR TO HIS *FABLED* SKILL WITH A *SWORD!*

YOUR MOVE, DOG!

SO CONTEMPTUOUS -- SO FULL OF SNARLED *DISDAIN* IS THE BRONZE-SKINNED BARBARIAN'S HURLED TAUNT--

--THAT THE BLOND ATTALAN FINDS HIMSELF *RESPONDING*, BY LEAPING WITH A BLOOD-CURD-LING *ROAR* A-CROSS THE SLAB, AS HE *SLASHES* IN MID-AIR!

IT IS A *BRAVE* MOVE IN ITS WAY -- A *FOOLHARDY* ONE IN MORE IM-PORTANT ONES--

BUT, MOST *SIGNIFICANTLY* OF ALL--

YYYY

--IT IS HIS *LAST!*

HE IS *DEAD*-- BE IT HELL OR A LAND OF FACELESS SHADES --BEFORE HE *STRIKES* THE *COLD STONES* AT THE *CIMMERIAN'S* FEET.

CONAN DOES NOT EVEN *LOSE STRIDE* -- BUT, THE *FOLLOWING INSTANT,* TURNS TOWARD --

ABLAH! YOUR *BARK* HAS BEEN *LOUD* THIS NIGHT.

NOW WE'LL SEE IF *YOUR* BITE IS *GREATER* THAN *MINE.*

S-STAY *BACK!!*

CURSE YOU, OUT- LANDER! I'D HAVE BEEN A *RICH* MAN WITH WHAT HUN-YA-DI *PROMISED* ME!

MAY YOU *BURN* IN *HELL- FIRE!*

IN HELL- FIRE PER- *HAPS!* I'LL LEARN THAT WHEN I *DIE.*

BUT *NOT* IN THE FIRE OF THAT ILL-AIMED *TORCH!*

YET, AS THE FIRE- BRAND HITS THE FLOOR, IT *SCATTERS SPARKS* FOR A MO- MENT-- THEN, THE ROOM PLUNGES INTO *DARK- NESS* --

-- AND CONAN'S *THIRST- ING SWORD* DRINKS NOTHING BUT THE *STILL NIGHT AIR.*

WHEN HE *RE-LIGHTS* THE SPUTTER- TORCH, THE ROOM IS *EMPTY,* SAVE ONLY FOR *HIMSELF* --

EMERGING FROM THE CHAMBER, HE FINDS HIMSELF IN A *NARROW STREET*, WITH THE STARS FADING FOR DAWN.

NOT FAR AWAY, HE SEES THE DARKENED HOUSE OF PERI-DICCAS...

...AND INSTANTLY WONDERS HOW MUCH OF A HAND BARDYLIS AND HER FATHER HAD IN TONIGHT'S PLOT.

HE DOES NOT LIKE TO THINK THAT THE GIRL HE SAVED HAS *BETRAYED* HIM... AND YET...

...HE MEANS TO *FIND OUT!*

BUT, HE HAS SCARCELY REACHED HER DOOR, WHEN--

OH, CONAN! WHAT HAS HAPPENED?

I--I FOUND YOUR CHAMBER *EMPTY* A SHORT TIME AGO WHEN I-- I WENT TO *LOOK IN* ON YOUR SLUMBER, AND--THERE WAS *BLOOD* ON THE COUCH!

ARE YOU *UNHURT?* NAY THERE IS A *CUT* UPON YOUR SCALP..!

IS THERE? I DIDN'T *NOTICE.*

IN A FEW WORDS, CONAN *EXPLAINS* WHAT HAS HAPPENED-- YET, TRUSTING *NO ONE* IN THIS STRANGE VALLEY, HE ADDS A FEW *EMBELLISH-MENTS* OF HIS OWN:

THIS *ABLAH* -- HE'S NOTHING, JUST A *PERSONAL ENEMY* OUT TO SETTLE A FEW *OLD SCORES* LEFT OVER FROM OTHER DAYS IN *MESSANTIA.*

MESSANTIA? YES--I THINK I'VE *HEARD* OF THE PLACE.

YOU *SHOULD!* IT'S THE CAPITAL OF ARGOS.

WHAT *MATTERS* IS THIS *SHAME* UPON MY HOUSE--MY *FATHER'S* HOUSE!

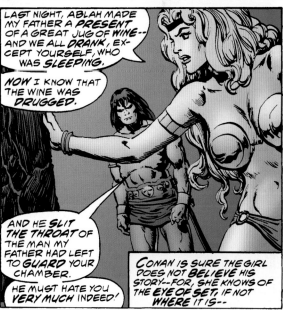

LAST NIGHT, ABLAH MADE MY FATHER A *PRESENT* OF A GREAT JUG OF WINE-- AND WE ALL *DRANK*, EX-CEPT YOURSELF, WHO WAS *SLEEPING.*

NOW I KNOW THAT THE WINE WAS *DRUGGED.*

AND HE *SLIT THE THROAT* OF THE MAN MY FATHER HAD LEFT TO *GUARD* YOUR CHAMBER.

HE MUST HATE YOU *VERY MUCH* INDEED!

CONAN IS SURE THE GIRL DOES NOT *BELIEVE* HIS STORY--FOR, SHE KNOWS OF THE *EYE OF SET*, IF NOT *WHERE* IT IS--

--AND, HE'LL BE GLAD TO GET *RID* OF IT, COME THE DAWN.

JUST THEN--

YOU! OUT-LANDER!

NOW WHAT THE *DEVIL*--?

PTOLEMY THE GREAT WOULD SEE YOU.

THAT HE *WILL*-- COME *MORNING*.

HE WANTS TO SEE YOU *NOW*!

THEN LET HIM TROT OVER *HERE*! CROM KNOWS, HIS *LEGS* ARE LONG ENOUGH.

YOU WOULD *BLASPHEME* ONE WHO IS A DESCENDANT OF THE *GENERALS OF ISKANDER*?

BY *ZOOS* WE'LL TAKE HIM IN *PIECES* IF WE MUST!

I NEVER HEARD OF A GOD OR DEMON NAMED *ZOOS*-- BUT IF IT'S A *FIGHT* YOU WANT--

--I'VE *OBLIGED* THAT KIND OF REQUEST FROM *CIMMERIA* TO THE *COASTS OF KUSH*, AND I SEE NO NEED TO STOP *NOW*!

NO! STOP IT, ALL OF YOU!

THIS MAN IS A *GUEST* OF MY FATHER'S HOUSE --AND HE'LL BE TREAT-ED AS SUCH!

BUT *PTOLEMY* SAYS TO *BRING* HIM-- SO WE *MUST*!

AYE! IF WE FAIL, *PTOLEMY* WILL *CRUSH* US IN HIS BARE ARMS --AND *SMILE* AS OUR BONES CRACK!

A FINE *IMAGE*-- BUT I THINK I'LL JUST COME *WITH* YOU TO PTOLEMY.

IF THERE ARE BONES TO BE BROKEN IN THE LIGHT OF DAWN, I'LL BE WANTING *MY* SHARE.

THE *SUN* IS JUST RISING AS THE TWO GREEK SOLDIERS ESCORT THE BRONZED FOREIGNER INTO THE *PALACE OF ATTALUS*... BUT ALREADY, THE *PEOPLE* OF THE CITY ARE UP AND ABOUT...

...AND *MANY* OF THEM FOLLOW THE PROCESSION, AS IF HUNGRY FOR THE *VIOLENCE* WITH WHICH IT MAY END.

MUCH BECOMES *CLEAR* TO CONAN WHEN HE SEES THE *VULTURE-LIKE* FIGURE WHICH HOVERS BEHIND THE SEATED *BLOND GIANT*...

ABLAH! YOU WASTED PRECIOUS LITTLE *TIME*, I'LL SAY *THAT* FOR YOU!

SILENCE, OUTSIDER! MAKE YOUR *CHARGE*, TRADER.

AYE, GREAT PTOLEMY...

I ACCUSE THE BARBAR- IAN OF -- *MURDER!*

THIS MORNING BEFORE DAWN, HE *ATTACKED* MY FRIENDS AND MYSELF WHILE WE *SLEPT* -- AND *SLEW* THE ONE WHO LIES HERE.

THE *REST* OF US, HERE, BARELY ESCAPED WITH OUR *LIVES!*

WHAT HAVE *YOU* TO SAY, BARBARIAN?

THAT HE'S A *LYING DOG!*

YES, I *KILLED* THAT MAN --

AT THIS, A *FIERCE CRY* ERUPTS FROM THE GATHERED *MEN OF ATTLUS* --

-- AND CONAN KNOWS HE IS ONLY A *HAIR'S BREADTH* AWAY FROM THE *MISGUIDED VEN- GEANCE* OF THE *MOB!*

THAT STYGIAN AND HIS ATTALAN LACKEYS SLIPPED INTO MY *CHAMBER* LAST NIGHT AS I SLEPT IN THE *HOUSE OF PERDICCAS* --

-- KNOCKED ME SENSELESS, AND CARRIED ME AWAY TO *ROB*, AND *KILL* ME!

HE SPEAKS THE *TRUTH*, GREAT PTOLEMY!

THEY ALSO SLEW ONE OF MY FATHER'S *SERVANTS*, WHO GUARDED THE GUEST-CHAMBER DOOR.

A *LIE*, O PTOLEMY! BARDYLIS IS *BEWITCHED*!

BEWITCHED, YOU SAY? *HOW*?

IS THE OUTLANDER *OTHER* THAN THE *SIMPLE BARBARIAN* HE SEEMS?

HE IS A *WIZARD*!

I KNOW HIM OF *OLD*! BEWARE, GREAT RULER OF THIS CITY!

HE WILL BRING *MADNESS* AND *RUIN* UPON ATTLUS IF HE IS NOT *SLAIN* AT ONCE.

HMMM. I HARDLY KNOW *WHICH* OF YOU TO BELIEVE; I TRUST *NO* OUTSIDERS.

THEN HEAR *THIS*, O PTOLEMY: *THAT ONE* SAID HE CAME AS AN *EMISSARY FROM HARAKHT*--YET PRODUCED *NO EVIDENCE* OF THE FACT, AS HE WOULD HAVE IF HE SPOKE THE *TRUTH*!

THERE IS SOMETHING IN WHAT YOU *SAY*...

WELL, SAVAGE? WHAT SAY YOU TO *THAT* CHARGE?

I BRING YOU AN *EYE OF SET* FROM THE NEW KING OF HARAKHT-- BUT I PREFERRED TO *REST* BEFORE I PRESENTED IT TO YOU.

NOW THAT I'VE SEEN HOW *DENSE* YOU ARE, I WONDER IF MY TRIP HERE WAS WORTH THE *BOTHER*.

YOU VILE-TONGUED, BLASPHEMOUS *CARRION*!

YOU *SEE*? HE STANDS *CONDEMNED* OUT OF HIS *OWN MOUTH*.

LET *ME* HAVE HIM, O PTOLEMY, AND *TORTURE* HIM UNTIL HE--

NO! LET *NO MAN* DARE TOUCH THE BARBARIAN!

NO MAN, THAT IS, SAVE MYSELF, *PTOLEMY*--

YET, THE NEXT MOMENT, CONAN TURNS HIS FOE'S SHEER MASS TO HIS OWN *ADVANTAGE*--

--AS PTOLEMY PLUNGES *OVER* HIM, UNABLE TO CHECK HIS *VELOCITY!*

THEN, KNOWING THAT HIS *BEST* CHANCE IS TO PREVENT THE GREEK FROM *RISING*, THE NORTHERNER HURTLES ATOP HIM--

--HIS MIGHTY *FISTS* PUMMELING A JAW WHICH SEEMS AS HARD AND UNYIELDING AS THE *GRANITE BOULDERS* WHICH SURROUND THE VALLEY OF ISKANDER.

NOW, IT IS *MAN TO MAN*, FIGHTING AS THE PRIMITIVE *PROGENITORS* OF THE HUMAN RACE MUST ONCE HAVE FOUGHT...

...THE GIANT *PTOLEMY* CATCHING HIS ANTAGONIST IN A GRAPPLE WHICH THREATENS TO *SNAP HIS SPINE* LIKE A ROTTEN BRANCH!

ARMS LIKE *TREE-TRUNKS* LIFT THE SNARLING CIMMERIAN OFF THE VERY *FLOOR*...

BUT, CONAN'S LIMBS, THOUGH SMALLER, CAN LIKEWISE WRECK HAVOC, EVEN TO A HUMAN LEVIATHAN!

LIKE A WOUNDED BULL, THE ATTALAN MONARCH DROPS HIS BRONZED BURDEN--

--ONLY TO SURGE TOWARD HIM AGAIN, LIKE A LIVING TYPHOON WHICH, A MOMENT HENCE, WILL SWEEP ALL BEFORE IT IN ITS ELEMENTAL FURY!

CONAN SWAYS, UNEASY ON HIS FEET, HIS BREATH STILL COMING IN HEAVING GASPS...

HE SEES THE KING TOWERING ABOVE HIM, REELING, ARMS SPREAD.

HE SEES HIS FOE'S BELLY GOING IN, AS HE DRAWS A GREAT LABORING BREATH...

...AND SUDDENLY, INTO THE RELAXED PIT OF HIS STOMACH--

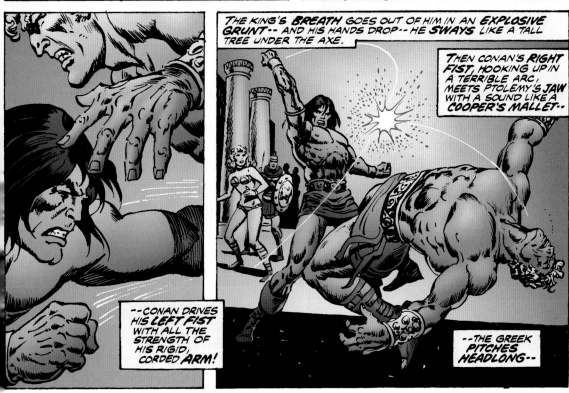

THE KING'S BREATH GOES OUT OF HIM IN AN EXPLOSIVE GRUNT-- AND HIS HANDS DROP-- HE SWAYS LIKE A TALL TREE UNDER THE AXE.

THEN CONAN'S RIGHT FIST, HOOKING UP IN A TERRIBLE ARC, MEETS PTOLEMY'S JAW WITH A SOUND LIKE A COOPER'S MALLET--

--CONAN DRIVES HIS LEFT FIST WITH ALL THE STRENGTH OF HIS RIGID, CORDED ARM!

--THE GREEK PITCHES HEADLONG--

-- TO LIE STILL.

FOR A MOMENT, MEN GASP, THEIR EYES FIXED ON THE PROSTRATE GIANT AND THE GROGGY, MASSIVE FIGURE THAT WEAVES ABOVE HIM.

THEN, THE SOUND OF STAGGERING FOOTSTEPS BREAKS THE TABLEAU--

--AND THOSE SAME EYES TURN TO THE SWAYING FORM THAT HAS APPEARED IN THE DOORWAY:

ARISTO! BUT--YOU WERE GUARDING THE PASS!

WHAT HAS HAPPENED?

S-STYGIANS--

THREE HUNDRED OF THEM! TH-THEY HAVE STORMED THE PASS--

--USE A KIND OF LONG BOW-- WE'VE NOT SEEN BEFORE--!

STYGIANS-- HAVE-- ENTERED-- THE-- VALLEY--!

I--

NO CLAMOR OF TERROR GREETS THE APPALLING NEWS... AND, IN THE UTTER SILENCE THAT FOLLOWS, BARDYLIS TURNS TO THE STILL-GASPING BARBARIAN IN THEIR MIDST...

YOU HAVE CONQUERED PTOLEMY.

HE IS EITHER DEAD OR SENSELESS.

NOW, YOU ARE KING. THAT IS OUR LAW.

TELL US WHAT TO DO!

AND CONAN FIGHTS BACK THE DEMONS WHICH ASSAIL HIS BRAIN, TELLING HIM TO SLEEP... TO DREAM.

HE HAS EVER WISHED TO BE A KING... AND FOR THIS ONE DAY, AT LEAST, IT SEEMS HE SHALL BE ONE.

A KING -- WHOSE CITY SEEMS DOOMED TO DIE!

NEXT ISSUE: AN EYE FOR AN EYE!

"Know, O prince, that between the years when the oceans drank Atlantis and the gleaming cities, and the rise of the sons of Aryas, there was an Age undreamed of, when shining kingdoms lay spread across the world like blue mantles beneath the stars.

"Hither came Conan, the Cimmerian, black-haired, sullen-eyed, sword in hand, a thief, a reaver, a slayer, with gigantic melancholies and gigantic mirth, to tread the jeweled thrones of the Earth under his sandaled feet."

—The Nemedian Chronicles.

Stan Lee PRESENTS: CONAN THE BARBARIAN™
THE EYE of the SERPENT

ROY THOMAS * HOWARD CHAYKIN & ERNIE CHAN * D. WOHL * A. GOODWIN
WRITER/EDITOR   ARTISTS/ADVENTURERS   LETTERS   CONS. EDITOR

YOU! AS *COMMANDER* OF THE VALLEY'S ARMY, WILL YOU ACCEPT ME BOTH AS *KING* -- AND AS *GENERAL?*

WHEN *ISKANDER* LEFT OUR ANCESTORS IN THIS VALLEY, LONG YEARS AGO, HE ALSO LEFT US *LAWS.*

WE OBEY THE *LAW OF ISKANDER.*

GOOD! I KNOW *ATTALAN* DOES NOT HAVE *MANY* MEN TO PUT INTO ARMS... BUT I DOUBT IF THE *STYGIANS* NUMBER MANY MORE.

I KNOW *WHO* IS BEHIND THIS INVASION -- THAT ONE-EYED DEVIL *HUN-YA-DI,* THE PRIEST WHO TRIED TO *KILL* ME AND OBTAIN THE *EYE OF SET* I BROUGHT HERE.

DOUBTLESS HE HOPES BOTH TO WIN THIS CITY'S *TREASURES* -- AND ALSO TO RETURN TO *HARAKHT* AND CROWN HIMSELF *KING* OF THE *HAWK-CITY,* TO BOOT!

WELL, WE'LL *SEE.*

GREAT CONAN -- WHAT OF THE *NEW BOW* WHICH KILLED THE GUARD?

WILL NOT ITS *GREATER RANGE* RENDER THE ADVANTAGE TO THE *STYGIANS?*

THEN WE'LL KEEP *OUT* OF BOW-RANGE... BEHIND ROCKS, IF NEED BE.

IF I KNOW *HUN-YA-DI,* HE'S SO HOT FOR BLOOD HE'LL SEND HIS MEN INTO *CLOSE ACTION,* THEN, RATHER THAN *WAIT US OUT.*

BUT *NOW,* BY CROM, GIVE ME MY BLADE -- ANY BLADE!

HERE, HEIR OF ISKANDER!

I DON'T MIND *HAND-TO-HAND* COMBAT NOW AND THEN -- BUT I NEVER FEEL AS GOOD AS WHEN I'VE A *HORSE* BETWEEN MY KNEES AND A GOOD *BROADSWORD* IN HAND.

MILORD -- WHAT WILL YOU DO WITH DEFEATED *PTOLEMY?*

JUST LEAVE HIM *HERE.*

HE *LIVES,* IT SEEMS -- BUT THERE'S NO TIME TO SEE IF MY BLOW *SNAPPED HIS BRAIN* OR NOT.

HE'D MAKE A *WORTHY* FOE -- ESPECIALLY FOR ONE WHO'S NOT SPENT HIS *WHOLE LIFE* FIGHTING OTHER MEN'S BATTLES.

I'VE LEARNED TO LIVE BY MY *WITS* AS MUCH AS MY *STRENGTH* -- AND THAT GAVE ME THE *VICTORY.*

AS THE CIMMERIAN HAS EXPECTED, THE TRADER *ABLAH*, WHO SET *PTOLEMY* AGAINST HIM, HAS *VANISHED*... BUT CONAN HOPES THEY'LL MEET *AGAIN*.

SOON, ARMOR-LESS BECAUSE THERE IS NO ARMOR IN THE CITY TO READILY FIT HIM, CONAN LEADS THE *WARRIORS* OF *ATTALUS* THRU THE *ILL-REPAIRED GATES.*

OFTEN HAS HE DREAMED OF BEING A *WARRIOR-KING;* BUT NOW, AS HIS DREAM BECOMES TRUE, IT IS NOT *PRIDE* HE FEELS, NOR *ARROGANCE*... BUT ONLY THE NAGGING WEIGHT OF *RESPONSIBILITY*...

... THE *BURDEN* OF ALL THE *LIVES* THAT REST HEAVY ON HIS *BROAD SHOULDERS.*

HE *WONDERS* FOR AN INSTANT IF THIS IS WHAT IT MEANS TO BE A *KING* OF MEN. THEN--

SOME DISTANCE AWAY, HE CAN SEE THE *DUSKY-SKINNED HORDE* SWARMING OUT OF THE *PASS* BEYOND AND INTO THE *VALLEY.*

THERE THEY ARE--

--THE *STYGIAN DOGS!*

DRUNK WITH *EXULTATION,* THE INVADERS HAVE *HALTED* TO SET *FIRE* TO THE OUTLYING *HUTS,* AND CONAN COUNTS HIMSELF AND THE ATTALANS *LUCKY MEN INDEED.*

ELSE, THE DYING SOLDIER *ARISTO* MIGHT NEVER HAVE REACHED THE *CITY* AHEAD OF THE STYGIANS THEMSELVES.

A DEEP RUMBLE OF RAGE ARISES BEHIND CONAN AT THE MURDEROUS, WANTON DESTRUCTIVENESS OF THE STYGIANS...

FOR, THE HILLMEN, MANY OF THEM SECRETLY RECRUITED BY HUN-YA-DI IN RECENT DAYS BY THE SHEER PROMISE OF BOOTY, ARE MAD WITH THE LUST FOR GOLD AND SLAUGHTER, SPARING NEITHER MEN--

--NOR WOMEN!

THEN, CONAN SEES HIM:

HUN-YA-DI!

BUT, LOOKING NO LONGER LIKE A MAN OF THE GODS, BUT LIKE A CONQUEROR-- A SCOURGE OF MEN AND DIETIES!

KILL THEM! KILL THEM ALL!

LET NOT ONE STONE STAND UPON ANOTHER IN ATTALAN WHEN THIS DAY'S WORK IS DONE!!

AND CONAN KNOWS, IN THAT SECOND, THAT A MAN MAY POSSESS TWO EYES, OR ONE, OR A THOUSAND-- AND STILL BE LESS THAN HUMAN!

BUT **STILL**, THE ATTALANS **HOLD THEIR FIRE**...

YOU'D **WASTE YOUR ARROWS** AT THIS RANGE.

WAIT TILL THEY COME **CLOSER!**

THEN YOUR PRECIOUS CITY ISN'T IN ANY **DANGER**, IS IT?

BUT, NEVER FEAR-- **THEY'LL COME--**

--OR I'VE LEARNED **NOTHING** IN SEVEN YEARS AMONG **CIVILIZED MEN!**

BUT, OUTLANDER-- **HIGHNESS**-- WHAT IF THEY DO **NOT** DRAW NEARER?

YOU **SEE**, LADS? THE JACKAL IS **IMPATIENT** FOR HIS **BOOTY.**

NOW **KEEP DOWN!** MAKE THEM COME **CLOSER STILL!**

BEFORE THE STYGIANS ARE **IN RANGE**, HOWEVER, IT IS **HUN-YA-DI** HIMSELF WHO FIRES A TAPERING **BOW--**

AND, EVEN AS HE LETS FLY AN **ARROW**, CONAN CANNOT HELP BUT WONDER HOW HE MUST HAVE **PRACTICED** FOR LONG, SECRET MONTHS, SOMEWHERE ON THE **TEMPLE GROUNDS** IN DISTANT **HARAKHT.**

NOT **OVERNIGHT** DOES A **PRIEST OF THE HAWK-GOD** LEARN TO FIRE A SHAFT--

--WHICH COMES SO **NEAR** TO STRIKING THE ONE IT WAS **MEANT TO SLAY!**

YYYAAA

NEVER WOULD CONAN HAVE BELIEVED, UNTIL THIS DAY, THAT A **ONE-EYED MAN** COULD BECOME SUCH AN **ARCHER!**

AT THE **SIGHT** OF THEIR FALLEN BROTHER, A **MUTTER OF IMPATIENT RAGE** RUNS ALONG THE LINE OF ATTALANS...

I'LL GIVE THAT DEVIL AN **ARROW** WHERE ONCE HIS **EYE** WAS!

NO!

YOU'LL TAKE ORDERS FROM **ME,** OR SO HELP ME CROM, I'LL **CUT OFF** THE HAND THAT HOLDS YOUR BOW!

SENSING THAT THIS NEW-CROWNED **BAR-BARIAN KING** MEANS WHAT HE SAYS-- THE ARCHERS **ONCE MORE** HOLD THEIR FIRE.

FOR LONG SECONDS, STYGIAN-AIMED ARROWS **CAROM** HARMLESSLY OFF THE GREAT BOULDERS WHICH HIDE THEIR ATTALAN FOES.

THEN, WITH A **BLOODTHIRSTY YELL** AS IF FROM A **SINGLE, IN-HUMAN THROAT**-

--THE **HILLMEN** STORM PAST, THEIR CITY-BORN, TEMPLE-BRED **MASTER**--

--AND **NONE** CAN SAY FOR SURE IF HIS SHOUTS ARE URGING THEM **ONWARD,** OR **CURSING** THEM FOR OFFERING THEMSELVES UP AS **LIVING TARGETS!**

AND **CONAN,** CROUCHING AMONG THE STONES, **GLARES** AT THE GAUNT, DUSKY FORM RUSHING TOWARD HIM UNTIL HE CAN MAKE OUT THE FANATICAL BLAZE OF THEIR **EYES.**

THEN--

FIRE!

NEXT INSTANT, A **THUNDEROUS VOLLEY** RIPS OUT ALONG THE WALL OF ROCK...

...AND **THIS** TIME, THE STYGIANS ARE **WITHIN EASY RANGE!**

MEN GO DOWN LIKE **HACKED REEDS** ALONG THE BANKS OF THE **RIVER STYX**...AND THEY DO NOT **RISE** THIS SIDE OF **DEATH.**

LOST TO ALL CAUTION NOW, AND SEEKING **REVENGE** FOR THEIR SLAIN COUNTRYMEN, THE ATTALANS **LEAP** OVER THE STONES TO HEW THE STAGGERING STYGIANS WITH **NAKED STEEL**...

AND, ROARING THE WILD WEIRD CRY OF THE **CYMMERIAN HILLS** WHERE HE WAS BORN-- **CONAN** DRAWS HIS SWORD AND **FOLLOWS** THEM!

NO TIME FOR *ORDERS* NOW... NO FORMATION, NO STRATEGY.

ATTALAN AND *STYGIAN*, THEY FIGHT AS MEN HAVE *EVER* FOUGHT-- WITHOUT ORDER OR PLAN--MASSED IN A STRAINING, GRUNTING, HACKING *MOB*, WHERE BARE BLADES FLICKER LIKE *LIGHTNING!*

THE RENDING OF *FLESH* AND *BONE* BENEATH THE CHOPPING SWORDS IS LIKE THE SOUND OF *BUTCHERS' CLEAVERS*--

THE *DYING* DRAG DOWN THE *LIVING*, AND WARRIORS *STUMBLE* AMONG THE MANGLED CORPSES.

MAN TO MAN, THE STALWART ATTALANS ARE MORE THAN A *MATCH* FOR THE *DARK INVADERS*-- AND THEY ARE FIGHTING FOR THEIR *HOMELAND*, THEIR *FAMILIES*...

...WHILE THE HIRELINGS OF *HUN-YA-DI* FIGHT AND PERISH ONLY FOR *GOLD* THEY WILL NEVER SEE.

AND *CONAN*?

WIELDING HIS DEADLY *BROAD-SWORD*, HE FEELS MORE AT *HOME* HERE AMID THE AGONY OF BATTLE THAN HE HAS FELT SINCE THAT MOMENT WHEN HE WAS SUDDENLY NAMED *RULER* OF A LOST RACE FROM A LOST, FORGOTTEN TIME...!

AND, THOUGH CONAN IS A **BORN FIGHTING-MAN**, EVEN HE CANNOT HELP WONDERING AT THE **MADNESS OF MEN**, THAT THEY DIE TO WIN **ANOTHER MAN** A JEWEL SUCH AS THE **EYE OF THE SERPENT-GOD SET**.

HE STOPPED LONG ENOUGH AT THE **HOUSE OF PERDICCAS** TO RETRIEVE THE GEM--AND NOW IT RESTS BENEATH HIS **BELT**.

NO ONE WILL HAVE THE JEWEL HE IS TO PRESENT TO THE **CITY OF ATTALUS** ITSELF--EXCEPT IT BE OVER HIS OWN **HACKED AND LIFELESS BODY!**

AS HE HEWS HIS WAY THRU THE FLAILING BLADES, HE MEETS ONE AFTER ANOTHER OF THE HIRED **HILLMEN**...

ONE BY ONE, HE **SLAYS** THEM...

...TILL HE SEEMS MORE LIKE THE **GREY REAPER** OF NORTHERN LEGEND THAN LIKE A **MAN** AT ALL!

FOR A FLEETING **MOMENT**, AMID THE SLAUGHTER, HE ALMOST **FORGETS** THE WHY AND WHEREFORE OF ALL THE **BLOOD-LETTING**.

BUT ONLY FOR A MOMENT.

THEN, HE SEES--

HUN-YA-DI!

YOU! YOU DOG OF A CIMMERIAN!

ARROWS HAVE FLOWN LIKE **BIRD-FLOCKS** THIS DAY, PRIEST--AND STILL WE BOTH **LIVE!**

STEP IN, THEN, AND TRY **COLD STEEL!**

DONE, BARBARIAN! I MATCH *MY* LIFE AGAINST THE *SERPENT'S EYE*, AND AN *ANCIENT THRONE!*

CONAN HAS FACED *MADMEN* BEFORE-- AYE, AND NOT A FEW OF THESE HAVE BEEN *PRINCES* AND *PRIESTS*, AS WELL.

RATHER, IT IS THE *DARK, LOOMING ABYSS* WHICH HE SUDDENLY *SENSES,* SOMEHOW, WHERE ONCE SAT AN *EYE*-- AS IF THAT EMPTY SPACE WOULD BE FILLED WITH *UNSPEAK-ABLY EVIL POWER* IF THE LONG-LOST EYE WERE REPLACED BY A CERTAIN *ORB-SHAPED GEM!*

THUS, IT IS NONE OF *THOSE* ASPECTS OF CRUEL-MOUTHED HUN-YA-DI THAT GIVES THE CIMMERIAN *PAUSE* FOR A CRUCIAL INSTANT.

PERHAPS, CONAN TELLS HIMSELF, THERE IS EVEN *MORE* AT STAKE THIS DAY THAN A *CROWN!*

THEN, WITH A *WILD LAUGH,* THE STYGIAN SWINGS HIS BLADE IN A *BRIGHT SHIMMER OF METAL* WHICH CATCHES THE MORNING SUN!

IT IS *WELL* FOR CONAN THAT HIS *WRIST* IS A SOLID MASS OF UNYIELD-ING CORDS-- THAT HIS *EYE* IS QUICKER AND SURER THAN A FALCON'S-- THAT HIS *BRAIN* AND *THEWS* ARE BOUND TOGETHER AS *ONE*...

FOR, *INTO* HIS ATTACK, HUN-YA-DI BRINGS *SKILL* SUCH AS HE COULD SCARCELY HAVE LEARNED IN A *HUNDRED YEARS*--

--UNLESS IT WERE TAUGHT TO HIM BY *DEMONS* CONJURED UP ON MOONLESS NIGHTS FROM SOME *REPTILE-INFESTED CATACOMB,* DEEP BE-NEATH THE BOWELS OF THE *HAWK-CITY!*

TWO SWORDS SPARKLE THERE IN THE SUNLIGHT--

THEY GRIND TOGETHER--

--LEAP APART--

--LICK IN AND OUT LIKE LIVING THINGS!

ONCE, THE STYGIAN'S BLADE GLANCES OFF HIS FOE'S BRACELET, TO CATCH THE OUTLANDER'S ARM-- AND A TRICKLE OF CRIMSON BEGINS.

BUT, THERE IS NO WORD-- NO OUTCRY--

--NO SOUND BUT THE RASP OF FEET ON THE ROCKS... THE RAPID WHISPER OF THE WEAPONS... AND THE DEEP PANTING OF THE TWO MEN.

STILL UNRECOVERED FROM THE FIGHT WITH GIANT PTOLEMY, CONAN FINDS HIMSELF THE HARDER PRESSED OF THE TWO.

THOUGH HE HURLS THE STYGIAN BACK TIME AND AGAIN, IT IS AS IF SOME IN-HUMAN SOURCE FEEDS ENERGY TO HIS GRIM OPPONENT.

CONAN FEARS NO MAN IN A FAIR BATTLE-- BUT AGAINST THE WRATH OF SERPENT-GODS AND DEVILS, WHO CAN STAND?

HIS LEGS TREMBLE NOW, AND HIS SIGHT BLURS--

--AS HE CLOSES ONE LAST TIME WITH THE UNTIRING MAN OF SET.

AS IF THRU A MIST HE SEES THE TRIUMPHANT SMILE GROWING ON HUN-YA-DI'S THIN LIPS...

NEXT MOMENT, THE STYGIAN IS *DOWN*--

--CLUTCHING THE *AIR* WITH TWITCHING HANDS, AS IF SOMEHOW TO PULL HIM *UP* AGAIN!

HIS EYES ARE *GLAZED* NOW, HIS LIPS *DISTORTED* IN A GHASTLY SMILE, AS HE CHOKES OUT HIS *FINAL WORDS*--

TO-- THE *MISTRESS*-- OF ALL-- *TRUE ADVENTURERS!*

TO-- THE LADY-- *DEATH*--!

THEN HE *SINKS BACK* AND LIES STILL, HIS PALLID *FACE* TURNED TO THE SKY...

NOW *MER-ATH* SITS SECURELY AT LAST ON THE *THRONE OF HARAKHT!*

NOT THAT *I* CARE MUCH, EITHER WAY-- BUT A *VOW* IS A *VOW*--

AND NOW, I CAN DELIVER THE *SERPENT-EYE* TO--

WHAT THE DEVIL?

BLOOD-- DRIPPING FROM BENEATH MY *LOIN-CLOTH!*

DID THAT JACKAL *WOUND* ME THERE WITHOUT MY *FEELING* IT--

--OR IS THE CAUSE-- *SOMETHING ELSE??*

EVEN *BEFORE* HIS HAND REACHES BENEATH HIS BELT, CONAN *KNOWS* THE ANSWER--

YET, IT IS THE EVIDENCE OF HIS *STEEL-BLUE EYES* THAT IS NEEDED TO TRULY *CONVINCE* HIM...

...THAT THE *SACRED EYE OF SET*...THAT *GEM BEYOND COMPARE*...

...IS *BLEEDING!*

CROM!

HE *RESISTS* A FLEETING URGE TO HURL IT *FROM* HIM, AS FAR AS HE CAN-- THEN THRUSTS IT *BACK* IN PLACE.

A *VOW* IS A *VOW*...

BUT, ALL THE SAME, HE'LL BE GLAD WHEN THE JEWEL IS IN *RIGHTFUL HANDS*, THE SYMBOL OF *PEACE* BETWEEN HARAKHT AND THE *LOST VALLEY OF ISKANDER!*

...WHERE THEY *HAVE NO CHOICE* BUT TO THROW DOWN THEIR *ARMS*...

SPARE US, MEN OF ATTALUS!

WE HAVE NO QUARREL WITH YOU, NOW THAT *HUN-YA-DI* IS DEAD!

MOMENTS LATER, THE *WOMEN* FROM THE VILLAGE BELOW, UNABLE TO STAY ANY LONGER FROM THE SCENE OF BATTLE, *BURST* UPON THE SCENE...

...AND *FOREMOST* AMONG THEM IS THE BLONDE BEAUTY CALLED *BARDYLIS!*

TO THAT END, HE NOW *RE-TURNS* TO THE FRAY BELOW...

...WHERE THE *LAST* OF THE STYGIAN HILLMEN ARE BEING *HERDED* BY FLASH-ING SWORDS INTO A STONY *CUL-DE-SAC*...

WILL MEN *EVER* BLAME *LEADERS* BECAUSE THEY THEMSELVES ARE BUT *FOLLOWERS*?

AND **ONE** THERE IS WHO STRIDES **GIGANTICALLY**, YET WITH **UNSURE STEP**, AMONG THE WOMEN WHO STREAM FROM THE CITY GATES...

IT IS **PTOLEMY**, ONCE RULER OF ATTALUS... HIS FEATURES GROTESQUELY SWOLLEN AND BLACKENED FROM CONAN'S IRON FISTS.

STILL, HE **WALKS**, CONAN CANNOT HELP BUT THINK... LIKE A **KING**.

AT ANY RATE, IT IS THE **GIRL** WHO REACHES HIM **FIRST**...

CONAN! ARE YOU **ALL RIGHT?**

--LIFE WOULD HAVE **GONE** ON.

IF ANYTHING HAD **HAPPENED** TO YOU--

ALL THE SAME, I'M **FINE**, AND GLAD **OF** IT!

PTOLEMY-- HAVE YOU COME TO **RENEW** OUR BATTLE?

I AM **NO CHILD**, TO HATE A MAN WHO HAS **BESTED** ME IN A FAIR FIGHT-- THEN SAVED MY **KINGDOM** WHILE I LAY SENSELESS.

NAY, I COME TO OFFER MY **HAND!** WILL YOU TAKE IT AS A PLEDGE OF MY **LOYALTY** TO ATTALUS' **NEW** KING?

I'LL TAKE YOUR **HAND**-- BUT I'VE DECIDED I **DON'T** WANT YOUR **CROWN.**

IT TAKES NO **SEER** TO KNOW THAT THAT WOULD KEEP ME **FOREVER** WITHIN THE BOUNDARIES OF THIS **VALLEY**...

AND I'VE STILL **WANDERING** TO DO, BEFORE I FIND THE LAND **AND** THRONE THAT **SUIT** ME!

THE KINGSHIP IS **YOURS** AS A **TRUE** HEIR OF ISKANDER, **WHOEVER** HE WAS.

FOR AN INSTANT, A LOOK OF **SHOCKED SURPRISE** CROSSES PTOLEMY'S FACE. THEN, BECAUSE **MONARCHS** MUST CONTROL THEIR **EMOTIONS**, AT LEAST IN PUBLIC...

YOU HAVE GIVEN ME BACK MY **CROWN**-- AND I MEAN TO BE **WORTHIER** OF IT IN THE FUTURE THAN IN THE PAST.

HAH! ONE THING, AT LEAST, I KNOW FOR CERTAIN...

WHEN YOU **RETURN** TO THE COURT AT HARAKHT, I WILL **AGAIN** BE THE **STRONGEST MAN** IN THIS LOST VALLEY!

I REGRET THAT I DID NOT *RECOVER* MY SENSES IN TIME FOR THE *BATTLE;* I SAW ONLY THE *LAST* OF IT.

BUT, IF I DID NOT REACH THE *FIELD* IN TIME TO SMITE THE STYGIAN DOGS...

...I HAVE AT LEAST RID THE VALLEY OF ONE *RAT* I FOUND HIDING IN THE *PALACE!*

CASUALLY, THE BLOND GIANT TOSSES SOMETHING AT *CONAN'S FEET...*

IT IS THE SEVERED HEAD OF *ABLAH,* THE TRADER WHO HAD SUPPLIED *INFORMATION* TO HUN-YA-DI, AND *LIES* TO PTOLEMY HIMSELF.

IN THE LONG MORNING *SHADOWS,* ONLY THE *EYES* SHINE CLEARLY AT THE CIMMERIAN... AND THEY ARE *TRANS-FIXED WITH HORROR.*

HE HAD *WANTED* TO FIND THE *EYE OF SET* -- AND NOW HE IS *NEAR* IT, AS NEAR AS AS HE SHALL EVER *GET.*

THEN, INTO PTOLMEY'S *HAND* CONAN THRUSTS THE *EYE OF SET*, WHICH HE HAS GUARDED WITH HIS *LIFE* THESE PAST PERILOUS DAYS...

MY *THANKS*, OUTLANDER! THIS JEWEL IS A SYMBOL OF THE *GOOD WILL* BETWEEN HARAKHT AND ATTALUS-- TWO OF THE ONLY STYGIAN CITIES WHICH DO NOT FEEL THE *YOKE OF LUXUR* HEAVILY UPON THEIR SHOULDERS!

WHEN WE DESCEND THE HILL, YOU WILL TAKE THE *OTHER* "EYE" BACK TO *KING MER-ATH*, AS HAS BEEN OUR *CUSTOM* SINCE THE DAYS OF *ISKANDER* HIMSELF.

THEN THIS PART OF STYGIA CAN REMAIN AT *PEACE*.

I'M A *STRANGE* ONE TO HAVE BEEN PICKED FOR A TASK TO PRESERVE THE *PEACE*, PTOLEMY.

MAYBE IT'S JUST AS *WELL*, THOUGH-- SINCE THE LAST FEW DAYS HAVE BEEN ANYTHING *BUT* PEACEFUL...

...THANK CROM!

GOOD! THEN, LET US *GO*...

IN A *MOMENT*! I WOULD SPEAK WITH *BARDYLIS*.

AS YOU *WISH*.

THEN, WHEN THE RESTORED KING OF ATTALUS HAS *DEPARTED*...

BARDYLIS...YOUR *FEELINGS* FOR ME WARM MY *HEART*, BUT THERE IS SOMETHING I MUST--

YOU NEED *NOT*; I *KNOW*.

YOU HAVE A *MATE* BACK IN THE HAWK-CITY... A WOMAN CAN ALWAYS *TELL*.

SHE IS A *FORTUNATE* WOMAN, BEYOND ALL *BELIEF*...

BUT *I* AM FORTUNATE, *TOO*-- IF ONLY FOR *TODAY*-- BECAUSE SHE IS *FAR AWAY*!

PERHAPS WE'LL BE *LOVERS* FOR A DAY, PERHAPS *NOT*... BUT, I *WARN* YOU, CIMMERIAN...

A *DAUGHTER* OF *ISKANDER* DOES NOT GIVE UP *EASILY*!

IF CONAN HAS A READY *ANSWER*, HIS WORDS ARE *LOST*, AS THE LIPS OF *BARDYLIS* PRESS AGAINST HIS OWN...

...AND A *HUNDRED CENTURIES* ARE SWEPT AWAY IN A BURST OF *FIRE* AND *PASSION*...!

THE END

... And the World Trembled Beneath His Feet

Personal Notes on Marvel's
Conan the Barbarian #72-77, 79-81
by Roy Thomas

Bêlit, Robert E. Howard's "Queen of the Black Coast," has long been intriguing to me—and, I suspect, to most other Conan aficionados, as well. After all, she was clearly the first great love of the Cimmerian's life—or was she? When she comes onstage for the above story, the only REH tale in which she is even mentioned, the white she-pirate's crew of black corsairs from the pseudo-African coast has just captured Conan. She is instantly smitten with and does her "love dance" for him, and he apparently makes love to her right then and there, on the deck of the *Tigress*.

But—what did Conan *really* think of her? Was he as smitten as she? Did their liaison truly grow into love—or did he merely do what he had to do in order to stay alive? After all, he couldn't be certain whether, if he overthrew Bêlit, her ebony buccaneers might turn on him rather than make him their new captain! Maybe he just, so to speak, rode the horse in the direction it was going.

When I fleshed out the Conan-Bêlit period from one short story to three-plus years' worth of comic-book stories, I decided to deal with the above, as well as with the matter of who she really was, and how she'd become a pirate queen. All that Howard had said about her—assuming we could take her word of it—was that her "fathers were kings in Asgalun." So I decided, in **CTB #72**, to have Bêlit journey to that city—with Conan at her side.

Asgalun (also spelled Askalon) was a city in Hyborian-age Shem, mentioned in two of REH's prose tales—"Queen" and "The Jewels of Gwahlur." As de Camp wrote in an exegesis of the names in REH's Conan stories, Howard probably derived it from that of Ascalon/Ashkelon, "an ancient city in Palestine." Using that as virtually my only Howardian building block, I constructed a back story for Bêlit which involved making old N'Yaga someone who'd been with her since childhood and who had fled with her when her king-father was slain—as seen in the previous volume of this series. Of course, REH may have meant only that Bêlit's *distant ancestors* had been kings—or just as likely, he never gave the matter any thought at all—but I came up with a scenario which I didn't think out of line with what Howard himself might have done, had he turned his mind one day to writing more about the buccaneer queen of the Black Coast. Actually, the story arc that begins in the first tale in this volume won't "pay off" unless an eleventh volume of **Chronicles of Conan** continues the reprinting of **CTB**.

(Incidentally, in the 1980s, another author *did* write a story about Conan's life with Bêlit. This was the eminent science-fiction and fantasy author Poul Anderson, who gave an entirely different origin for the she-pirate. But this was several years after I'd done Marvel's version, so even when I returned to writing **Conan** in the 1990s, I ignored Poul's paperback novel, since it would've been difficult to reconcile it with what I'd done earlier.)

"He Who Waits—in the Well of Skelos!" in **Conan the Barbarian #73** was based on a page-long outline by Howard that had been sent to me by the estate's literary agent, Glenn Lord. REH's "The Well of Skelos" was an outline for a story about pirates—perhaps one featuring REH's pirate hero Black Vulmea—who force a captive to lead them to a "Temple of the Toad," with fatal results.

The name "Skelos," used by REH in several Conan stories, refers to an ancient author of magical books. There are several mentions in the tales to "the iron-bound books of Skelos," as if being "iron-bound" somehow made those books more potent, more formidable—or maybe the iron binding was simply meant to help keep something imprisoned in its pages from escaping?

(Might as well mention here that Kawaku, the rebel pirate of this story, was named after a young lady named Annette Kawaki, who was studying to be a doctor and whom I dated briefly while she was doing a bit of lettering for Marvel. I'll bet she had what it took to get through medical school, and is now residing in luxury somewhere, and never dreamed that a comic book villain had been called after her surname!)

With **CTB #74** John Buscema and I took the *Tigress* to Khemi, a major port city of Stygia (the ancient Egypt of the Hyborian Age, which de Camp felt was probably named either after Khem, of an Egyptian fertility god—or after such ancient names for Egypt itself as Kamt, Kam, Chem, and Chemia—you pays your money and you takes your choice).

We also used that issue to bring Conan's Stygian arch-foe Thoth-Amon back into the fray, if only in a "dream" for the present. Actually, I was reluctant to have the Cimmerian meet Thoth in person earlier than he had in REH's stories, but I played around with it here. However, as a few readers pointed out later, it makes little sense for Thoth to assault Conan in a nightmare, then seem totally ignorant of the barbarian when the latter actually shows up in Stygia. "Was it someone else using Thoth's image to warn Conan away?" they asked me. I'd just wink, say "Maybe so," and walk away. To paraphrase the great Irish poet William Butler Yeats—when I wrote that sequence, only Crom and I knew what I meant. Now, only Crom knows.

Since Howard had written in "Queen" that "survivors of butchered Stygian ships named Bêlit [and the "white warrior" with her] with curse," the attack on Khemi and the burning of several Stygian vessels before her "black walls" were in keeping with REH's plan for Conan, such as it was.

With #75 I went a bit further afield with fantasy elements. As per the previous volume of this series, John and I had Conan, Bêlit, and corsairs fight the Dragon-Riders, men who rode on giant crocodiles. Now we created, as guardians of an inland Stygian city named Harakht, warriors who flew astride giant hawks—"Hawk-Riders." I knew I'd enjoy seeing John's handling of such a concept, as indeed I did—as did the readers. I asked John to carry on the fight between the Cimmerian and a raptor-piloting Stygian, then between the barbarian and the hawk itself, for several pages, and I loved writing every panel of it. I nearly gasped when I first saw the big panel on the fourteenth story page—in which we're looking downward past Conan and the plummeting raptor as the ground is coming up fast. Here again was a perfect example of what I always said about Big John Buscema: "He can draw anything you can get him to *think* about drawing!" We even tossed in a short croc-fight at the end. What I wanted to do here was show Conan as the ultimate survivor—the guy who takes everything you can throw at him—man, giant hawk, crocodile—and emerges triumphant at the end of the story, standing there with his dagger dripping blood and watching another giant hawk fly toward the hawk-city carrying the woman he loves. ("Harakht," by the way, is—if my memory serves me right—one way of spelling the ancient Egyptian named for the hawk-god whose moniker is usually given as "Horus.")

Conan and Bêlit also perform an act that will have far-flung repercussions when they take the slave girl Neftha from the Stygian ship they raid—but that plotline wouldn't bear its definitive fruit for a number of issues yet, and certainly not in this volume.

"Swordless in Stygia," in **CTB #76**, takes its name from a poem-drama called **Eyeless in Gaza**; I'd always loved the sound of the latter phrase. In this three-issue Harakht sequence, I was trying to write the equivalent of one of REH's short novels (or long short stories—take your pick), with a bit of intrigue thrown in. Howard has sometimes been called a simplistic writer, as if his plots were all cut from cookie cutters, but it ain't so—there are enough twists and turns in a Conan story like "People of the Black Circle," for instance, to make one's head spin.

This three-parter ended with #77's "When Giants Walk the Earth!"—about which I remember relatively little besides what's in the story itself. Hopefully, the tale speaks for itself, and made a fitting climax to the Harakht story arc.

At this point, we necessarily skip reprinting **Conan the Barbarian #78**, which was already a reprint of sorts—a tale from the first issue of Marvel's ultra-successful black and white mag **The Savage Sword of Conan**, "colorized" and slipped into the monthly comic in order to buy a little time while John Buscema moved on to another project and I worked with a temporary replacement. Because that story co-starred Red Sonja, it will have to wait for some sort of cross-company publication, hopefully, at a later date.

With **CTB #79**, the penciller of the series, for about half a year, became a young Howard Chaykin. (But hey, we were all a lot younger then.) Howard was already making a bit of a splash in the comics field, and we'd worked together on the 1976-77 adaptation-in-advance of the film **Star Wars**—but **American Flagg** and his other cutting-edge works were still ahead of him.

He and I hung out together occasionally in those days, and since he'd told me he could use a regular gig for a while, I invited him to draw pencil layouts for several issues of **Conan**. Looking at these pages, you won't see much of Chaykin, because embellisher Ernie Chan—just as he was asked to do—made the result look as much like usual Buscema/Chan art as he was able to do.

I decided to "tread water" for a few issues by having Conan take his leave of Bêlit in order to pursue an inland adventure. Not surprisingly, he encounters another wench or two over the next half dozen issues, and his relationship with the she-pirate, strong as it is, doesn't keep him from straying when a beautiful blonde named Bardylis pops up. I suppose I could have kept the Cimmerian faithful, but I just didn't see that as essentially part of his stormy nature. So sue me.

"The Lost Valley of Iskander" was "freely adapted," as I liked to put it, from a "modern-day" story written by Howard in the late 1920s or early 1930s. The original tale had starred one of REH's earliest creations, Francis X. Gordon, a.k.a. "El Borak"—a term that was supposed to mean "The Swift" in some Eastern tongue, though I suspect Howard simply made it up. The Gordon part of the name he probably took from the famed British commander "Chinese" Gordon, who was eventually killed at the nineteenth-century Battle of Khartoum—while "Francis X." seems likely to have been borrowed from silent movie star Francis X. Bushman. REH's stories of *his* Gordon are set in Afghanistan, where England and Russia then played what was called "The Great Game," each trying to conquer the country for their own purposes, mostly by gaining control of the strategic Khyber Pass. (Howard was a great fan of popular writer Talbot Mundy, author of **King—of the Khyber Rifles**, which has been made into a movie at least twice.)

Francis X. Gordon was, unlike most of REH's heroes, only of medium height. He was a soldier of fortune—a former gunman from El Paso, Texas, who roams the Middle East in the early twentieth century. Another Texan, Robert E. Howard, wrote over a dozen "El Borak" stories, counting several that weren't published until long after his death. "Iskander" was one of those, first seeing print in 1974, in a volume with exquisite illustrations by Michael Wm. Kaluta.

As for "Iskander"—it was nothing but an alternate version of the name of that far-famed Greek conqueror, Alexander the Great! Howard postulated that Alexander passed through Afghanistan on his way to India—as indeed he'd almost certainly have had to—and left behind there a city called Attalus, populated by several hundred of his soldiers and the native women they took up with. Since no one was likely to connect the name "Iskander" to "Alexander," I didn't see any reason to change it when I did the Marvel/**Conan** version spread over three issues—but, to inject an element of fantasy (as I tried to do in *every* Conan story I scribed), I revealed that Iskander was Alexander! Somehow, walking into the mists of this mountainous land, Alexander had journeyed back in time and had founded a Grecian dynasty 10,000 years before he was even born. Rod Serling would have been proud of me, I reckoned.

I added the Eye of Set, I believe, in order to give Conan a proper quest to be on.

My one regret in the story is that I didn't change the name "Ptolemy," which was the true historical name for the Greco-Egyptian ruling house in early-A.D. Egypt, whose members were descended from Alexander's generals. The last of the Ptolemies, in fact, was the famous Cleopatra, of Julius Caesar and Marc Antony fame. But I don't recall anyone complaining.

And there we leave Conan, in mid-quest—and in mid-Chaykin. Will the quest be resumed in another volume? We'll all have to wait and see, won't we?

Roy Thomas wrote Marvel's Conan the Barbarian, Savage Sword of Conan, **and** King Conan **comics from 1970 through 1980, then again from circa 1990 until Marvel relinquished the franchise at the end of that decade. He also co-scripted the second Arnold Schwarzenegger movie,** Conan the Destroyer, **and has scripted the swashbuckling Cimmerian in several other media, as well.**

ALSO FROM DARK HORSE COMICS!

THE DARK HORSE BOOK OF WITCHCRAFT

Featuring Mike Mignola, Tony Millionaire, Scott Morse, Evan Dorkin, Jill Thompson, and others; Cover by Gary Gianni

Mike Mignola's Hellboy faces the nature of monstrosity, Jill Thompson (*Scary Godmother*) and Evan Dorkin (*Hectic Planet*) return to their spectral pet adventures, and Scott Morse (*Soulwind*) presents a tale of old Salem.

Hard cover, 96 pages, Full color
$14.95, ISBN: 1-56971-935-7

HELLBOY VOLUME 1: SEED OF DESTRUCTION

By Mike Mignola and John Byrne

Dark Horse presents new editions of the entire *Hellboy* line with new covers, beginning with *Seed of Destruction*. *Hellboy* is one of the most celebrated comics series in recent years. Sent to investigate a mystery with supernatural overtones, Hellboy discovers the secrets of his own origins, and his link to the Nazi occultists who promised Hitler a final solution in the form of a demonic avatar.

Soft cover, 128 pages, Full color
$17.95, ISBN: 1-59307-094-2

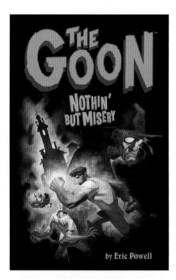

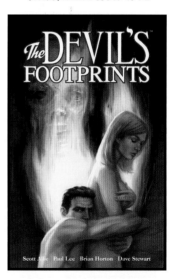

THE GOON, VOLUME 1: NOTHIN' BUT MISERY

By Eric Powell

An insane priest is building an army of the undead, and only one man can put them in their place: the Goon. This volume collects *The Goon* issues 1-4 and *The Goon Color Special*, originally published by Albatross Exploding Funny Books; presented in full-color for the first time.

Wizard Magazine says, "Every comic should be this much fun to read!"

Soft cover, 136 pages, Full color
$15.95, ISBN: 1-56971-998-5

THE DEVIL'S FOOTPRINTS

By Scott Allie, Paul Lee, Brian Horton, and Dave Stewart

Brandon Waite investigates his dead father's study of witchcraft. But his desire to protect loved ones forces him to cover up his own tentative steps into the black arts, leading him to mix deception with demon conjuration, isolating himself in a terrible world where his soul hangs in the balance.

Soft Cover, 144 pages, Full color
$14.95, ISBN: 1-56971-933-0

AVAILABLE AT YOUR LOCAL COMICS SHOP OR BOOKSTORE • To find a comics shop in your area, call 1-888-266-4226
For more information or to order direct visit **darkhorse.com** or call 1-800-862-0052 • Mon.-Sat. 9 A.M. to 5 P.M. Pacific Time
*Prices and availability subject to change without notice
Mike Mignola's Hellboy™ © 2004 Michael Mignola.

ALSO FROM DARK HORSE

CONAN VOLUME 1 THE FROST-GIANT'S DAUGHTER AND OTHER STORIES

Collecting the first seven issues of the all-new hit series by award-winning writer Kurt Busiek (*JLA/Avengers, Astro City*) and dynamic artists Cary Nord, Thomas Yeates, and Dave Stewart. In this handsome 192-page collection, Conan wars with the murderous Vanir, meets the Frost-Giant's Daughter, and is taken as a slave by the ancient sorcerers of Hyperborea!

ISBN: 1-59307-301-1
$15.95

CONAN PVC SET THE FROST GIANT'S DAUGHTER

The Frost Giant's Daughter PVC set is the first of a series of sets of non-articulated PVC figures based on the Conan stories by Robert E. Howard. Each set features exquisitely detailed sculpting and painting. Figures designed by noted artist Arthur Suydam. Conan stands approximately 4" high; the giants are a massive 7" high.

ITEM NO.: 12-659
$44.95

CONAN THE SLAYER

Sculptor Jeffery Scott, well-known for his long tenure at Gentle Giant Studios, has captured the true essence of Conan. Exacting in its details, this piece brings forward a sculptural interpretaion of Conan that delivers the goods, and then some. 7" high, packaged in a deluxe full-color box, limited edition.

Item No.: 12-708
$49.99

CONAN LUNCH BOX

Now you may enlist the aid of Robert E. Howard's celebrated Cimmerian to help you carry your lunch. Featuring artwork by Barry Windsor-Smith, considered by many to be the ultimate Conan artist, this lunch box would serve any barbarian proudly!

ISBN: 1-59307-225-2
$14.99

AVAILABLE AT YOUR LOCAL COMICS SHOP OR BOOKSTORE
To find a comics shop in your area, call 1-888-266-4226
For more information or to order direct visit darkhorse.com or call 1-800-862-0052
Mon.-Fri. 9 A.M. to 5 P.M. Pacific Time
Prices and availability subject to change without notice

Conan® and Conan the Barbarian® are trademarks of Conan Properties International, LLC.

ALSO FROM DARK HORSE

CONAN THE BARBARIAN
MINI-BUST

Following the success of our first Conan mini-bust, this piece features Robert E. Howard's immortal warrior intertwined in a fearsome death struggle with a gigantic snake. 7" high, packaged in a deluxe full-color box, includes certificate of authenticity.

ITEM NO.: 12-812
$49.99

ROBERT E. HOWARD'S VALERIA
MINI-BUST

Robert E. Howards's classic story "Red Nails" introduces Valeria, a swordswoman and buccaneer. Possessing a fatal beauty and a diamond-hard nerve, she joins Conan as an equal against a savage foe. Sculpted by Jeffery Scott. 7" high, packaged in a deluxe full-color box, includes certificate of authenticity.

ITEM NO.: 13-339
$49.99

AVAILABLE AT YOUR LOCAL COMICS SHOP OR BOOKSTORE
To find a comics shop in your area, call 1-888-266-4226
For more information or to order direct visit darkhorse.com or call 1-800-862-0052
Mon.-Fri. 9 A.M. to 5 P.M. Pacific Time
*Prices and availability subject to change without notice

Conan® and Conan the Barbarian® are trademarks of Conan Properties International, LLC.

ALSO FROM DARK HORSE BOOKS

THE CHRONICLES OF CONAN
By Roy Thomas, John Buscema, Neal Adams, and others

VOLUME 5:
THE SHADOW IN THE TOMB
& OTHER STORIES
ISBN: 1-59307-175-2 / $15.95

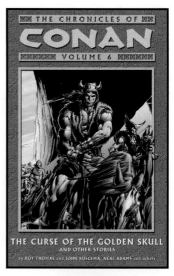

VOLUME 6:
THE CURSE OF THE GOLDEN SKULL
& OTHER STORIES
ISBN: 1-59307-274-0 / $15.95

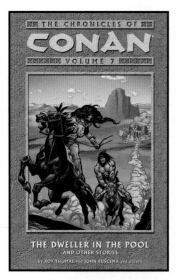

VOLUME 7:
THE DWELLER IN THE POOL
& OTHER STORIES
ISBN: 1-59307-300-3 / $15.95

VOLUME 8:
BROTHERS OF THE BLADE
& OTHER STORIES
ISBN: 1-59307-349-6 / $15.95

AVAILABLE AT YOUR LOCAL COMICS SHOP OR BOOKSTORE
To find a comics shop in your area, call 1-888-266-4226
For more information or to order direct visit darkhorse.com or call 1-800-862-0052
Mon.-Sat. 9 A.M. to 5 P.M. Pacific Time
*Prices and availability subject to change without notice

Conan® and Conan the Barbarian® are trademarks of Conan Properties International, LLC.